End to End

*The beauty is in the walkings- we are
betrayed by destinations.
~ Gwyn Thomas*

Happy Trails !

Seth + Lyssa + Tina

ISBN 978-1-4951-7866-5

Published by
six!dogstudios
2120 Forebay Road
Pollock Pines, CA 95726

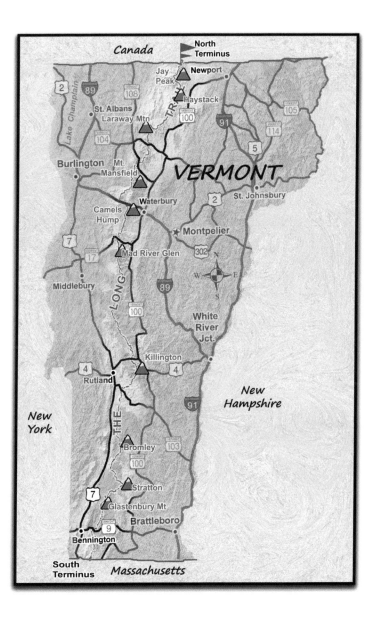

Table of Contents

Preface

Sept 10, 2016

Day 9
Bamforth Ridge, Vermont

A little before 5:00 I woke up to flashing lights and crashing booms. For a moment I thought I had stumbled into the firing range again. Then I realized that a thunderstorm was fast approaching, and I decided it would be prudent to make a mad dash out to pee before it hit. Lyssa and Tina had the same idea, and together we dashed out to do our business in the bush. Tina and I dove back into the tent just as the rain started, but Lyssa did not. I stuck my head out of the tent to call her but by then the storm was on us and my voice was drowned out by the rain and crashing thunder. I tried counting the number of seconds between lightening strikes and thunder rolls, but there was no gap at all. The cell was directly overhead!

(I'm not really a writer. I am a veterinarian and I spay cats for a living. In 2016, at the age of 58, I drove 3500 miles across the country, leaving my job, my husband and 6 dogs at our home in the Sierras. I drove to Vermont with 2 dogs and did a 3 week back packing trip on the Long Trail, a 275 mile walk down the spine of the Green Mountains. And then I came home. This is my story.)

My Long Trail Journey began with a 4 day drive from Pollock Pines, California, to North Troy, VT. I started the morning of August 29th, 2016, with my trail companions Tina and Lyssa. Tina is a 9 year old mixed breed terrier with a heart murmur, and Lyssa is a 5 year old 85 pound German Shepherd. We are all experienced hikers, having done the Tahoe Rim Trail, parts of the PCT and miles of hiking in the Sierras. Tina had just seen her cardiologist who said she was stable and doing well on her medicine, and gave her a green light to go with me on the hike. I have 6 other dogs and naturally they all wanted to go, but Tina and Lyssa are the friendliest and also the most obedient and bonded to me. They are both strong, agile, and energetic, and passionately enthusiastic about hiking. Lyssa can carry 6 days worth of dog food for herself and Tina without batting an eye.

The cross-country drive went well and 4 days later I arrived in Williamstown, Massachusetts. I needed to pick up a package of last minute gear from the Williamstown Post Office. The package was due to arrive first thing on the morning of September 2nd, so I decided to camp out and maybe go for a hike if there was time up at Clarksburg State Park (north of North Adams). This turned out to be a great idea and the girls and I had our first taste of hiking on the east coast- the forest was green and there was water everywhere- puddles, little brooks and waterfalls, ponds, bogs and mud puddles! There were lots of colorful mushrooms, loads of moss, and delightful things like salamanders and frogs! This was why I came to New England to hike. I love Northern California, but we were in the grip of a serious ongoing drought. Trails were dry and choking with dust, streams and lakes were drying up and the threat of wildfire was constant. There was often a pall of woodsmoke in the air, obscuring the view and impairing one's ability to breath. Trees were dying from the combined stress of competition for moisture and a plague of bark beetles. It was enough to break this tree-hugger's heart. I craved wetness and greenery and the Green Mountains sounded like the perfect antidote for the dry and dusty blues.

(Spoiler Alert)
Unlike the fine book by Cheryl Strayed, there are no drugs or sex in this story. I'm more about dogs than drugs. And honestly, I value a good pair of socks more than sex. The closest thing I have to offer to hallucinatory drugs is a couple of pretty good endorphin highs. And I did meet a trail angel who was pretty loose with his egg sandwiches. I took a picture of him and shared it with a girl-friend

when I got home. She said he was "hot." I hadn't noticed. I only had eyes for the sandwich. Sorry. In my defense, I did come out of my shell quite a bit, sociability-wise. My friendly four-footed companions helped with that. They tend to break the ice with most folks. But more than that, making friends with people on the trail is easy because the trail becomes home, and other hikers therefore become family. So no sex, but definitely some warm fuzzies.

This is a story about being a late middle aged woman facing the reality that my years of good health and easy mobility are foreseeably finite, which was not the case even 5 or 10 years ago. It's a story about traveling 7000 miles with 2 dogs as my constant and wonderful companions, about appreciating the gift of their incredible friendship and what they brought to the journey, and about understanding the terms of their commitment to me- their needs and my responsibility for them. Lastly it's a story about processing the deaths- and the lives- of my Mom and Dad. Of honoring them by reclaiming my own life. (End Spoiler Alert)

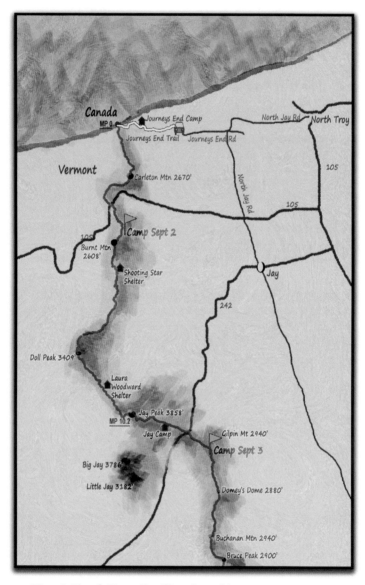

Map 1: North Troy, Trailhead parking area, Journey's End Camp, and The Canadian border.

Chapter 1

September 2, 2016

Starting

I began the day at the Post Office in Williamstown, and then set the compass to the North. After months of planning and anticipation I am finally ready to begin- today is the day! Winding my way up Rt 30 I began to remember a previous long forgotten drive across Vermont almost 50 years prior. I was 8 years old and my family had just moved to New York State from the Midwest. My father took the family for a tour of New England, with a view to checking out some of those legendary Vermont ski resorts he'd heard so much about. Riding in the back of the old Ford station wagon, I'd been amazed at the endless rolling hills of green forest. I spent the trip imagining myself freely roaming in those seductive green hills, maybe as a cowboy or an Indian or a pioneer, living in harmony with nature. Those memories stayed with me, so deeply buried that I had not thought of them until I saw the mountains again rolling out before me, and then I realized that part of the reason I had chosen to come to the Long Trail of Vermont was because of a memory so deeply hidden that I was not even aware of it until I was here: an old and faded childhood dream to roam these hills and forests! I finally had the freedom and the resources to pursue that dream.

North Troy. I arrive at the end of Journey's End Road at

what appears to be the parking area. There is one other car parked. I park next to it and start pulling out all my gear; I have a lot of sorting and organizing to do before I can depart. I can't forget any piece of gear but I don't want to carry a single ounce more than necessary. After about 20 minutes another car pulls up- a young woman has come to meet her husband who is finishing up his 21 day through-hike. She dashes off up the trail for her reunion and a little while later she reappears with a tired bedraggled looking young man. The man looks reasonably athletic: not too thin and not limping or showing obvious signs of injury. That's good. He shrugs out of his mud caked shoes and peels off socks and proceeds to wring them out. That's not good. His feet are white and wrinkled and "jacked-up", in his words, with old blisters and callouses. Ugh. Dude- it's the dry season and it hasn't rained in a week- what's up with the wet feet? The trail is wet and muddy he says. It never, ever, dries out. Nothing ever dries out on this trail. Don't bother washing anything because you can hang it out for days and it will never get dry. The only way to get anything to dry is to wear it to bed, but it doesn't matter because it will just get wet again the next day. I gave up on being dry, he says. I just want a hot shower and clean clothes. And a beer. He looks at his wife. I give them some leftover junk food from my car trip and it is gone before they leave the parking lot. You'll have a fantastic time he says as he leaves- it's an incredible trail! (Note to readers- every thing he said about mud and wetness was true, but since I hate getting my feet wet I guess I was a little more careful about where I stepped- I never got wet feet. Or blisters!)

At 4:15 I am satisfied that everything is in it's place- gear, food, clothing, maps, cell phone, solar charger (ha!), first aid stuff. Lyssa's packs are loaded and balanced- she is carrying exactly 5 days worth of dog food for her and for Tina- carefully calculated and measured- along with rations of freeze dried 100% organic turkey jerky for treats. I

The Canadian Border

lock the car, double check it one last time and carefully stash the key deep in a hidden safe spot in my pack. It's been a long trip already, just getting to the beginning of this hike. We start walking. We are not hiking on the Long Trail yet- this is just the approach trail to the Canadian border where the official marker stands. A few hours later and I am standing there too, marveling at the fact that Canada is only one step away. I can step out of the United States and into a foreign country just like that! And back again. What if an alarm goes off, or I get zapped like those dogs that live in yards with invisible fences? My girls are waiting, looking to me for direction. I head south. Southbound, we roll!

I really like this trail. The forest is cool and quiet and moist and, well, very green. Exceedingly green. There is present every shade of green in the spectrum, more than could ever be described or named. Occasionally there is a boulder of pure white quartz, or a brilliant red berry seductively presented on a trillium platter, or a perfect

Northern Terminus

13

neon orange toadstool straight from a fairy tale. Their colors only accentuate the green-ness of the green of this forest. The trail is steep and rocky for sure, but I can do it. Nothing my modestly athletic middle aged muscles can't handle.

All too early the daylight started to show signs of fading. I checked the time- only 6:00- I should still have had another hour and a half, I thought. I was still fresh and full of energy, and had planned on making it to Shooting Star shelter for the night. I had a tent and so I didn't really need the cover of the shelter; the problem was that I had seen nothing resembling a flat or level bit of ground large enough to accommodate my tiny tent. Moreover, the forest was a jungle of thick shrubby vegetation and moss, littered with tangles of dead branches, tree trunks and rocks. I wanted to get as far as I could because I was counting on having a little "head-start" in order to meet my tight time schedule for finishing the Trail. At the last minute I had commit-

Trillium

14

ted myself to finishing the trail two days earlier than I had originally intended- 21 days instead of 23. Every day would count. On the West Coast I often was able to hike until 7 or 8:00 in the evening with plenty of light. We had open forests and big open skies, and long lingering sunsets. I never used a headlamp, and never missed having one. I pushed on. But before long it was obvious that soon I would not be able to even see the trail. It would be easy to trip and get hurt- how dumb would that be to do on my first few hours out on the Trail! I needed to find a place to stop and set up camp quickly, or I'd end up thrashing around in that brush in complete darkness! Near the top of Burnt Mountain the trail began to level out. I picked the first level spot I could find away from the trail, and cleared away just enough debris to pitch my little tent and spread out my sleeping bag. Tina immediately claimed the bag while Lyssa assumed lookout duty nearby. I fed the dogs and then sat down to make my own dinner- potato soup with parmesan cheese. I had barely enough water for the soup. Oops. We had crossed a half dozen streams on the way in, so the dogs were well hydrated, but I had neglected to think ahead to make sure we had enough water to get through the night and next morning. I didn't know when or where the next water source would be. Suppressing a spike of anxiety I poured the remaining half liter of water into a pot for the dogs and settled in for the night. I'd be up and on the trail super early in the morning, I thought. We'd be fine. The forest was very wet; there were plenty of little creeks and puddles, and we were all well hydrated. No worries.

No worries. I was nearly 4,000 miles away from home in a strange dark jungle of a forest, with a flimsy tarp over my head and out of water. The forest was nearly silent. An occasional squeak or creak disturbed the silence with new and sudden menace; Lyssa was on high alert. I turned on my solar flashlight and studied the guidebook. I guessed I'd made it about 3.5 mile in from the trail head at the Canadian border, near the summit of Burnt Mountain.

Shooting Star Shelter was less than a mile away. There should be water there, I thought. I could make it there for my morning coffee. Then there'd be a few miles of gradual uphill to Doll Peak at 3409', some downhill to Laura Woodward Shelter at about 2,800', and then the big climb of the day- a 1,000 foot ascent up Jay Peak. The contour lines on the map looked close together, which meant it was going to be steep. But this was a ski resort, I thought, how bad could it be? Besides, I'd done thousand foot climbs in full pack before at much higher elevations. So far so good, I assured myself. I had a nice head-start and I only had to make 10 miles tomorrow in order to keep to my itinerary. After months of work and planning I was finally on the Trail! No worries. I turned out the light.

September 3, 2016

Day 1
Jay Peak

The first night I camped in the forest near the top of Burnt Mountain, which is neither burnt, nor very much of a mountain. I thought I might make it to the Shooting Star Shelter, but I am not hiking as fast as I thought I would or it gets dark earlier than I thought it would. Later I realize the truth of the matter is that in Vermont the miles are longer and the days are shorter than on the west coast! Honest! It wasn't easy to find a 8' x 8' level patch of ground, but by 6:30 the gloom was deepening to the point where I would have to turn on a light or risk tripping over something. At the last minute I spotted a patch not too far off the trail. Normally I would have picked a spot well hidden away from possible passers-by, but I took a chance that no one else would be coming along in the dark....

I was so thrilled to be finally on the trail- backpacking with my beloved dog/friends in the Green Mountains- it was a miracle that I got any sleep at all. Lyssa barked once at something during the night, but otherwise it was quiet and peaceful. I set my alarm for 5:30, but Lyssa woke me up at 5:15, as is her habit. She is as reliable as your grandfather's clock. By the time it was light enough to see, we were packed up and on the trail again, having left no trace (at least as far as my senses could detect. Lyssa probably could find some traces.)

It took over an hour to take down the tent, feed the dogs, and organize my pack for the day. Terrible, I scolded myself. And that was without making coffee or oatmeal! I'd have to do better if I was going to make it to the finish line on time; I needed every minute of daylight for walking. But I also had to stay organized and not loose anything at the campsite. I had to keep us safe.

Finally we were hiking again. It felt wonderful! The dogs leapt and scrambled up the steep parts, ran ahead, and then ran back to see if I was coming. I was coming, and they dashed ahead again. If only I could show my friends in California what this forest is like- pictures and words weren't enough- you had to walk in it- breath in the scents and feel the cool dampness in your skin. Even the sunlight was different- soft and filtered. It was if we'd woken up on a different planet, or unknowingly stepped through one of those secret leprechaun passages in the old Celtic mythology. I was in Ireland in the time of elves and fairies. I was in Middle Earth. I looked around for a unicorn. The only thing I saw was my German Shepherd grinning at me from ear to ear. That was magical enough!

Before long I arrived at the Shooting Star shelter, where I planned to cook up a cup of coffee and study the map for a bit. The water pump at the shelter was broken or perhaps had gone dry- at any rate there was no water to be had from it. Shit, already I was in trouble! I needed coffee! Intending to move on, I hoisted my pack, but as I struggled with the straps I heard Lyssa slurping noisily from a puddle in some rocks not too far beyond. Water! Beautiful, brilliant dog! I scooped up enough water for my coffee before Lyssa drank it all. I didn't know whether the puddle was from a rainstorm or a semi-dried up creeklet but I was accustomed to hiking in the Sierras where water could be scarce and in a pinch we often made do with a puddle. I always filtered it, of course.

Just as the water came to a boil the girls announced the arrival of company! A northbound hiker, on his last leg of finishing the trail. He was the first human I'd seen since setting foot on the trail yesterday afternoon. I pumped him for information, which he was happy to share. He'd started the Trail over a year ago, but had to quit due to a bad fall coming down Ethan Allen Peak, 100 miles to the south of here. He'd torn a ligament in his knee and had to be helped off the trail with the assistance of some volunteer Rangers. Now he was back, and finally about to finish the journey. Like me, he'd discovered the joy of ultralight packing- it was the only way he'd been able to continue hiking, given his injury. I could have sat and talked about ultralight gear all day. But the most outstanding tip from this guy was instant peanut butter! I'd never heard of it. I watched in drooling fascination as he spilled a dollop of water into a zip lock bag with unidentified brown powder, squished it around, and spread it on a bagel. Peanut butter! I craved peanut butter every day for the next 3 weeks, and when my brother picked me up at the end of the trail I told him to be sure to bring a jar of peanut butter. (He did, and I ate it all.)

Energized by the coffee, I zoomed along the next few miles of rolling forest, feeling invincible. Lyssa and Tina were in heaven too, running back and forth, sniffing and investigating all the wonderful forest scents and sounds. Then we came to Jay Peak. The honeymoon was over.

Traditionally most backpackers hike the Long Trail from South to North, and the narrative in the guidebook is written as if you are heading north. I had chosen to go from North to South because the Northern sections had sounded more wild and pristine, and of course more physically challenging with the highest peaks and steepest climbs, and if in turned out that I was not able to do the whole trail I wanted to make sure that I at least got to do the most interesting and scenic parts. This meant that I was following the guidebook backwards; when the book said "ascend", I had to read it as "descend". "Climb up" translated to "climb down." "Climb up steeply" translated to "get ready to slide down on your butt and grab hold of anything you can." I wasn't sure what "descend steeply" translated to, but any rock climber knows that down-climbing is always harder and more dangerous than climbing up. Here's what the guidebook had to say about the Long Trail on the north side of Jay peak: *"From the tramway station, drop northeast on a ski trail, then turn left and cross another ski trail at right angles. Pass*

View from Jay Peak
Most visitors took the tram.

through a snow fence and cross a water pipeline, then enter the woods and turn right to descend steeply to Ullrs Dream ski trail. This trail drops 1.0 miles east to the Jay Peak Ski Area base lodge and Vt 242. Bear left to follow the north edge of this trail and the reenter the woods. Descend near the top of the ridge to Laura Woodward Shelter." I had to read this backwards. From Laura Woodward ascend to a ridge-top. In the woods. Follow a trail on the north edge. Then ascend. Steeply. In the woods, apparently. For awhile. Then cross pipeline just after you get out of the woods, then a snow fence. "Cross another ski trail at right angles"...that was confusing...should I cross it at left angles? Then another turn to another ski trail... "drop northeast....." means...what is the opposite of "drop?" Undrop? Undrop southwest on a ski trail.... to a Tramway Station! OK! All I had to do was try to stay on the trail, keep going up, and if all else failed I could just head for the Tramway Station. I couldn't miss that.

Jay Peak was my first hint that the guidebook has a tendency towards understatement. The day turned into a blur of endless steep rocky up and up and up, boulders, rocky ravines and gullies, finding cracks, ledges,

Lyssa is my self-appointed scout toeholds, hand-holds, roots,

20

saplings and trees with their bark polished by thousands of hikers grasping hands, holding on, balance, step up again, use my pole like a third leg to balance, pivot, propel my body and this pack which was never this heavy until it had to be lifted up against the force of gravity- could it be that gravity is like an elastic band and the further you stretch away the harder it pulls you down? No, I took physics; that's not how it works! Somewhere on the way up Jay Peak I stopped ro-

Our first summit

manticizing and decided that this was one tough m*****r of a trail. I'm not too proud to admit; Jay Peak kicked my butt and made me humble.

When I finally stepped out of the steep forest and onto the summit there was what I can only call a paradigm shift.

Imagine the sound of gears clanging and crashing as the set changes and the curtains rise, and I have stepped into a Fellini movie! At the Tramway Station a bride in white linen and lace is posing with a dozen bridesmaids for a pho-

tographer who is lugging a mountain of equipment and there is a very smiley woman with a clipboard who immediately begins to tell me about her corgi, or maybe it was a husky, who also loves to go hiking and isn't it just wonderful to be here! Wow. Not expecting this! A little girl attaches herself to

Jay Peak was a popular place for wedding receptions!

21

my shepherd like a bee to a flower, which fortunately is just fine with Lyssa, who knows that little girls often taste like cookies.

I ask the little girl to take our picture for me so I can show my brother that I am really here and now he can see what Jay Peak looks like in the summer time because he has only seen it in the winter when he goes skiing. I call Hank. Then we go down. And down and down. I bypass Jay Camp and cross the road and continue on because I am greedy for miles. I want to make 10 miles because the guidebook said that a reasonably fit hiker should expect to make 10 miles a day in the rugged north section of the trail and I imagine myself to be reasonably fit.

I needed to prove myself to be reasonably fit. I needed to imagine that I have a chance of finishing this Trail. I didn't figure out the cause of this compulsion until much later-I just went with it. Jay Camp would have been a lovely, logical and perfectly reasonable place to stop for the night after having climbed Jay Peak, especially on the first day of a trip. But it was only about 8 miles from where I camped on Burnt Mountain and I knew I had a few more hours of daylight, so I pushed on.

It was getting late in the day by the time we crossed Highway 242, and we were out of water again. The guidebook mentioned a spring on the south side of the highway. We needed to find it or we were in trouble. If we didn't find it or it turned out to be dry....I didn't want to even think about turning back. Luckily the spring was full and beautiful and Lyssa had no trouble finding it and thoroughly availing herself of the fresh cold water by the time I caught up to her. I filled up all of the water containers, adding a good four pounds of weight to my load. We needed water for dinner and breakfast, plus the 4.5 mile hike to Hazen's Notch Shelter, which was the next known water source. Then we started climbing again. The pack felt vastly heavier and every step up was exhausting work. Who would expect 2 liters of water to make such a difference! There is literally no spot level enough to set up camp for the night without rolling down the hill and so we had no choice but to keep climbing until we reached the south summit of Gilpin Mountain. We'd done 9.2 miles. The summit was a fairly level plateau, and probably the only level place to camp for miles around. The brush was thick and there was no view, but it would have to do. There was enough daylight to bushwhack my way off the trail to a secluded spot to set up the tent. The dogs knew the drill- eat, sleep, leave no trace. One day down, 20 to go.

Daylight faded into quiet, impenetrable blackness. It was just me and Lyssa and Tina in the remote, wild, northern mountain wilderness. Not another soul in the world. We were far enough off of the trail that possibly no one would ever find us. There was no cell signal, no email, no FaceBook, no news feed. I felt alone but not lonely. The quiet was a healing quiet; the peace was profound. I listened to the silent forest and let go of the fact that I was a world away from home.

I am a veterinarian by trade. Been one for half my life. For the past 15 or 20 years I have worked in private non-profit organizations doing mostly spay and neuter surgery. I started working with the local animal shelter early in my career. I'm the type of person who likes to help out when I can, especially if it seems like it's a good person who is asking for the help and the cause is deserving, and especially if it involves animals in need. Helping people who like to help animals in need became my dharma, and my specialty. After 5 years in private practice I had found myself totally demoralized by the commercialism- I felt like my whole career path had been a big mistake. Discovering shelter work gave me a reason for continuing in the profession.

I was never very keen on private practice. When I was a younger and much more idealistic version of myself, applying to vet school, all I wanted to do was help wildlife. Not long after I earned my degree I came to the realization that the most effective way to help wildlife was by leaving them alone and protecting their habitat. Once I wanted to become a zoo vet, but my ambitions had devolved to simply wanting to fence off vast areas of land, off-limits to humans, and release all of the caged and captive wild animals into it. Like, give them half of the earth, at least, just for the animals. This notion grew after several years of working with wildlife rescue organizations. Most of the animals who came in were victims of habitat disturbance and the actions of humans in appropriating animal homes and territories for "development" and commercial gain. There was no safe place to release rehabilitated animals. It only seemed fair to me that we should share the planet with all the other species who occupy it. Less people, more room for wildlife. Do the math.

There wasn't much I could do by way of reducing human population. However there was one route open to me wherein I could help reduce animal suffering and help make the world a little safer for wild animals, and that was through spay and neuter of dogs and cats. I turned out to be pretty good at it, and I enjoyed it. For many years, the time I spent helping shelters and doing spay and neuter was only a minor sideline to my "real" bread & butter work in private practices and emergency clinics. But gradually the animal rescue community began to embrace the value of spay and neuter as being an essential tool for curbing dog and cat overpopulation and reducing euthanasia rates. The field of shelter medicine was invented and blossomed into a bona-fide specialty. I accepted all opportunities to work as a spay & neuter surgeon. Eventually I was able to fill my schedule with surgery, and with no regrets or love lost I dropped out of "for-profit" practice altogether.

What a relief it was! For 14 years I had struggled to find happiness working in private practice. In truth, I worked in commercial practices mostly because of the bills: student loan payments, rent, car, groceries, gas, and then a mortgage, property taxes, insurance, house maintenance, clothes, computers, etc & etc! I felt like a rat trapped on a treadmill. I hated getting up in the morning. I fantasized about going back to school and finding another profession. Together with my husband Hank, a gentle soul who loved to sing and play the guitar, we set up a music store. Hank minded the store while I continued working in vet clinics to pay the bills until the store became profitable. The plan failed, trapping me even more deeply in the financial rat-race. The only thing that saved my veterinary career was my willingness to spay and neuter cats and dogs. In large numbers. For hours on end, and never grow tired of it. Plenty of shelters and rescue groups were willing to pay decent competitive salaries to people like me, because we were few and far between. Obsessive oddballs, really. But mainly, working in shelters suited my personality. Fundamentally I am not a "people person." I relate emotionally to my dogs far better than I do to people, including those close to me. I just want to help animals and so I am better suited to shelter medicine than anything else in the wide spectrum of veterinary careers. Not to say that shelter work is free of stress, politics, frustrations and plenty of people doing things out of poor judgment, ignorance and misguidedness. But at the end of the day I always felt like I have done a good days work and helped to make the world a better place, if only for several dozen homeless cats and dogs. And when I need it, I can take time off.

2016 marked my 28th year as a practicing veterinarian. As much as I battled against it, I was beginning to feel the aches and pains and ravages of 58 years of wear and tear on the body. Stiffening joints, fuzzy eyesight, diminishing capability to solve problems, learn new tasks, or comprehend an article in the journal (say it's not so, Mr. Wizard!) The clock, as they say, was ticking. Damn that clock, anyhow. Ever since I was a kid I'd dreamed about someday taking a long distance backpacking trip, but the opportunity had never presented itself. Now I was finally on the trail, doing it, and better late than never. I felt a little nervous about the adventure I was getting myself and the dogs into, but mostly I was exhilarated.

The South Summit of Gilpin Peak was the best place in the world to be in that moment. We were safe, and everything was under control. We were on track. One day down, 20 more to go. I could rest. Tina was curled up on my coat and tucked in by my shoulder, and Lyssa was a fortress of warm earth-scented fur parked across the front of the tent. There was no place on Earth I'd rather have been. By flashlight I studied the guide book and the map for the next 10 miles- the elevation profile looked like a jagged set of shark's teeth.

September 4, 2016

Day 2
Haystack

The morning is a roller-coaster: Domey's Dome, Chet's Lookout, Buchanan Mountain, Bruce Peak and Sugarloaf Mountain. The lower elevation forest is open, green, cool and pleasant for hiking. I can tick off these minor summits, hills really, with satisfying expediency. The morning goes well. I think about the upcoming major ascent of the day, Haystack Mountain. It occurred to me that I might handle the 2 miles of steep uphill better if I take a little refreshment break right before I start the climb, so I aim for lunch at Hazens Notch camp, 4.5 miles from my morning starting point. I will take my time and cook up a pot of soup and maybe wash a bit of laundry while I eat. And shampoo my head just to top things off.

A kindly looking man who reminds me very much of Radagast the Brown in the Lord of the Rings movie is spreading ashes in the campfire ring as Lyssa, Tina and I come bouncing in to Hazens Notch. Pungent fumes drift about and Radagast looks at me sheepishly and murmurs something

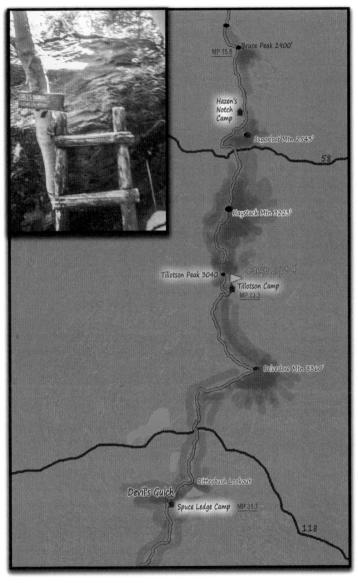

Map 2: Hazen's Notch Camp, Haystack Mountain, Tillotsen Camp, & Devil's Gulch.

about it being a chilly morning and some people think it might be an early winter. I notice he is wearing a Green Mountain Forest Ranger patch on his overcoat and I am curious about it, but he says he's off duty, really, and wishes me a blessed hike as he toddles off up the trail. OK then.

Refreshed and full of carbohydrates, I was zooming along once again on the approach to Haystack. But in case I had forgotten how steep and rugged the climb up Jay Peak had been, the Trail had a little reminder in store for me. Haystack Mountain humbled me anew, instilling in me more genuine respect for this trail. The climb begins by ascending up a steep gully of bare jumbled rock.

I surmised that the trail was not always a gully, nor were the rocks always so exposed. Soil and vegetation once covered everything. The problem is that the path was routed straight up the fall line. The mountaineers who laid out the trail did not know about switchbacks, or at least they evidently didn't believe in them. In the West our trails are never built like this, because we know what will happen. Within a few years the repeated impact of hikers boots compacts the soil, kills the vegetation and

its roots which hold the soil, and create channels for the flow of water down the slope. During rainstorms or during the runoff from the spring snow-melt the channels grow and wash away the soil. The surface of the trail drops below the level of the surface of the adjacent forest floor. Hikers must now climb up bare bedrock faces, favoring the edges where they can cling to saplings or vegetation for balance.

The Haystack Trail (I think)

The saplings break and the vegetation is uprooted and dies. The trail widens. More hikers come along and create a network of bypasses, trying to avoid the difficult and dangerous scramble up or down the steep, slippery rock. It's a mess.

I stood at the bottom of what appeared to be a wide vertical chute of bedrock slabs, tilted crazily in all directions. Was this really the trail, I wondered? What if I was lost already! There were no white blazes in sight. Lyssa and Tina ran ahead, agilely leaping and scrambling up from rock to rock. Then ran back down to see if I was coming. Show-offs! Not having a blaze in sight always made me nervous; if I didn't see one soon I would start to feel a little tingle of panic. Maybe I should just follow the dogs-they usually knew where the right trail was. Usually. Or should I backtrack to the last blaze and try again? Often the blazes were few and far between, and it was easy to mistake a patch of light colored lichen for a faded blaze. There was nothing else that looked remotely like a path. I started up. Slowly. Remembering the story of the hiker who had fallen and torn his ACL, I proceeded carefully up the rock, securing each toehold and using my pole for balance. Some sections were so steep that I tossed the pole up to the next ledge and grabbed onto rocky hand-holds or nearby unlucky sacrificial saplings with my hands to hoist myself up. Once or twice I ended up following false trails leading around impossibly steep boulders and had to backtrack when I realized I was lost in a tangled spiderweb of trails created by hikers who had made the same mistake as I did, trying to find an easier way around an obstacle. As we got further from the hikers' parking lot on Highway 58 the trail became more well defined and easier to navigate.

The challenge of staying on the trail might have been fun except that I had another problem. My potato soup was not sitting well in my stomach. Ominous waves of queasiness were beginning to grow, weak at first, but getting stronger and more frequent. Something was rotten in

A small mudpit

the state of Denmark, my father would say. (Quoting Shakespeare, he claimed.) This wasn't right. This could be trouble. I reviewed everything that had gone into my stomach over the past 24 hours: Nutrigrain Breakfast bar (blueberry), Quaker Oats granola bar with chocolate chips, coffee, 4 ounces of tuna in a foil package, instant potato soup with chunks of parmesan cheese added to make it heartier, a liter of instant milk, some dried fruit, water- all filtered through my Sawyer Squeeze bag filter system. I wondered about the water. The squeeze bag filter system was new for me since my trusty old Katahdin had broken right before I left California. My hiker friend at the Shooting Star shelter had raved about the Sawyer; swore by it. What if I had used it incorrectly and accidentally drank contaminated water? I knew all about giardia, cryptosporidium, listeriosis and the various coliforms. It seemed unlikely that

I could have picked up any of those bugs, but if I had, my only hope was that my immune system would kick in and limit the infection. If it was something I had eaten, it couldn't be too bad. My diet seemed pretty simple and safe enough. I soldiered on.

Mushrooms and one muddy little dog paw

Haystack is only 3,223', but the trail climbs

1700' in a mile before leveling out, sort of, on the summit ridge. The ridge itself is rocky and rough and I had my first encounter with something called a "summit bog". Summit bogs were unique and totally new to me. I mean, who would expect to find a muddy bog on the top of the mountain? Bogs are supposed to be in lowlands, places where water drains into from above and then sits because the way out is plugged up. But in the Green Mountains the soil at the summits is extremely thin, if indeed there is any soil at all, and the bedrock is only a few inches below. The summits are frequently the only flat areas. The soil absorbs the water and it sits there on the level ground and can't drain because the bedrock is impermeable. And nothing ever dries out on this trail, as we know. Imagine a thick verdant carpet of club moss and a treasure trove of diverse exotic alpine plants. So lovely but unfortunately so fragile and so easily obliterated by just a few dozen hikers tromping on it, churning the soil into mud. The entire trail from one side the other turns into a churned up mud pit, boxed in by logs, rocks and vegetation. It requires a lot of effort, agility, and in my case, a strong dislike of getting my feet wet, to dodge the mud and stay clean and dry. Walking on the edges of the mud pits causes another problem- the both the trail and the mud tends to get wider. Fortunately for hikers and summit bogs, the Green Mountain Club provides an alternative: puncheons. Puncheons are heavy slabs of rough cut timber laid down on supports, usually in pairs, providing a footbridge across the wet, thin, easily mudified alpine soil and it's fragile and exquisite vegetation. The puncheon walkways on Haystack were built with heroic effort- these thick heavy planks are carried up by hand or hand hewn from forest nearby. The summit ridge on Haystack is almost a mile long, and mostly bog. I quickly learned to love puncheons. Walking on puncheons is delightful because walking across summit bog that is not churned into a mud-pit is magical: a bridge across a miniature fairyland. I decided right then that the best thing I could do to repay this trail for all that it was giving to me was to make a donation to the GMC to build more puncheons.

How many puncheons can you build for $500? 500 feet? a mile? Haystack needed a lot more.

Whether it was the unrelenting rocks or the unrelenting mud pits between the rocks, or my unhappy bowels churning like the mud under a hiker's boots, Haystack was not particularly enjoyable. The only pleasant memory I have of Haystack was a conversation with another hiker about halfway up the mountain. She turned out to be a local resident, a dairy farmer from a small nearby town, who had moved here from Plattsburgh 30 years ago to start a farm. We talked about the Vermont dairy industry, the veterinary business, and the relative merits of living in North Eastern Vermont instead of the Western Slope of the Sierras. I'm not sure I would have wanted to trade places with her, and at any rate it wasn't an option. The summit was hot, humid and buggy, and there was no view, much to my disappointment. The only good thing about being on the summit was that there was a strong cell signal. I called Hank and gave him an update on my progress. It was not a particularly enjoyable conversation for either of us mainly because I was hot, tired, itchy and queasy. I also noticed that the charge on my phone battery had dropped much faster than I had expected so I cut the call short and scooted on down the mountain for Tillotson Camp. Only 2.7 miles, and all down hill, or so I thought. I should have studied the map harder.

Remember the elevation profile that looked like a jagged row of shark teeth? There was one more tooth to go. On the map it was overshadowed by the ugly fangs of Haystack, but Tillotson Peak was as steep and rugged as anything I'd encountered so far, and all the more challenging for being unexpectedly tacked on to the end of an exhausting day. Adding injury to insult, I capped off my ill-fated expedition over Haystack Mountain by failing to notice a broken off snag of a small sapling protruding from the ground near an 18 inch step down a boulder. Somehow the snag stabbed into my knee like a stiletto, leaving a nasty little laceration over my kneecap. Just what I needed. I slapped a band-aid on it to keep it clean and kept going.

Tillotson Peak caught me by surprise- a not so gentle reminder that this trail does not take prisoners! Having conquered the monster Haystack didn't we deserve a nice coast down to Tillotson Shelter? Guess again! The trail lulls you with a lovely serene beaver pond- it's so tempting to linger and watch for birds, or a glimpse at a beaver or moose which surely must frequent this pond. But the afternoon shadows are lengthening and I want to get to the shelter before dark. On we go and wham- around the bend the trail hits us with 500' of 'very steep' (i.e. straight up) heavily eroded bedrock. OMG. I can hear the Trail mocking me! "Silly westerner! How dare you belittle my peaks and ridges- only 3,000' indeed! I'll show you steep and rugged; I'll show you strenuous; I'll show you Mountains! You thought you were done for the day- Ha! Climb this, sucker!" Lesson learned: steep and rugged is rugged and steep at any elevation.

Tillotson camp rates a luxury 5-star lodge by Long Trail shelter standards. It is fully enclosed, with a screen door, bunk beds and a table. I stuck my head in the door for a quick peek, said hello to the hiker who had already staked out a bunk, and decided it felt claustrophobic. I pitched my tent a little ways apart from the cabin, and did my evening chores. Feed dogs, filter water, sort gear. Four more backpackers pulled in to camp. Rugged looking, ex-military type middle aged men, heavily loaded, moving fast and strong. I was really glad I hadn't chosen the cabin.

It was kind of a rough night. The men took turns getting up and going out to use the outhouse all night long; the screen door on the cabin creaked and slammed with every exit and re-entry. I had eaten a ration of tuna and some fruit even though I wasn't especially hungry, but I knew I needed the calories and protein. I laid in my sleeping bag half in and half out. I felt grubby and queasy and battered by the day. It was impossible to find a comfortable position. I had carefully cleaned and dressed my lacerated knee. I couldn't sleep. For the past few years I'd frequently found myself unable to sleep, especially in the small hours after midnight, and my thoughts would inevitably fall into a familiar well-worn track. I'd traveled that track so often that it had worn into a deep groove with sides so steep I couldn't climb out. It was a box canyon, a trap. The trail always led to the same conclusion: Dad died, Mom did too. I had done my best, made the best choices I knew how to make, but the end result was always that I couldn't save them.

Night after night I relived the past few years of my parents' lives, examining the events marking their decline into dementia and Alzheimer's disease, re-evaluating and questioning my decisions and actions. Was there anything I'd missed, anything I could have done differently? Should I have intervened earlier or been more assertive in assuming responsibility for their care? It was a bottomless pit of self-doubt but I couldn't stop torturing myself.

In some ways I had been heading towards that particular trail-head since I'd been born. But the mind trap of endlessly rehashing the past started etching itself in my brain when in 2015 I willingly exchanged roles with my Mom: I became caregiver and guardian and she became the dependent. Not my child, exactly, but child-like and progressively helpless, until at times I felt like I was caring for a 120 pound infant. She would have despised the thought that she was a burden to me, and so I told her over and over again how happy we were to have her with us. I wasn't lying. She was always sweet and kind, and I was crazy about her. The only problem was that they lived on the east coast and I lived in California.

My father gave Mom over to my care and keeping in January of 2015 when he finally found the door to the next world, the door for which he had long been yearning, and slipped through. His passing was unexpected only to those who were not privy to his private thoughts, which encompassed the vast majority of his social community, and to his doctors and nurses who couldn't find anything physically wrong enough with him to signal impending death. Until the last moment he was able to maintain his facade of the strong, capable, self-reliant Master & Commander of all he surveyed. He was determined to maintain his dignity and independence until the bitter end, and as usual, he got his way. We made suggestions: Dad, maybe you should at least get on the waiting list for assisted living (the thought of assisted living rendered him livid.) Dad, maybe you should take advantage of that visiting nurse that could come in a few times a day to help out with stuff (and covered by your insurance! He forgot he had insurance.) Dad, what about attending this support group meeting for people taking care of family members with Alzheimer's (he tried it and nothing they said made any difference: Mom just kept getting worse, he said.) Dad, how about calling that pastor you like so much and talking to him about that suicide dream you had. And so on. He adamantly refused all help.

The first time he fell and they found him on the floor in his apartment he was rational enough to convince them that he did not want to go to the emergency room. The second time he went down was only a few days later and he was delirious enough that the EMTs could override his protests and take him to the hospital.... where they could find nothing particularly wrong with him except that he was delirious and couldn't stand up without toppling over. "Vascular dementia," the neurologist said, "acute exacerbation must have hit his head when he fell." They had to tie his hands to keep him from pulling out the catheters and monitoring devices. Sedate him to keep him from trying to wander about and risk falling again. I knew why he was doing it. He absolutely did not want to be kept alive, to be "hooked up to a bunch of tubes", lying helpless and vulnerable, stripped of his dignity and control. We had often talked candidly about it and he had made me promise that I wouldn't let that happen. And absolutely he did not want to end up "on the hill", in the "loony bin", which was his name for the skilled nursing unit (christened the "Wellness Center" by the marketing department at their Senior living facility.) He knew it was a warehouse for people who were waiting to die. I promised him I'd never let him end up there. Like I had any control over it. I think he wanted me to put him out of his misery like I would a terminally ill animal who was suffering. Right. "You'd do it for a horse. Horses get better care than I do." You're not a horse, Dad.

The day before he was scheduled to be relocated to the Wellness Center he had surgery to place a permanent indwelling catheter in his bladder, which he never would have permitted had he not been delirious and at the mercy of his designated healthcare power of attorney, (i.e.- me. But there was no choice since his urethra was now almost completely blocked by scar tissue from previous prostatic surgery), and that night he found the door. And stepped through. To the vast relief of everyone except for his doctors and nurses who were still expecting him to be moved to skilled nursing that day. Dad had other plans. For the last few years the only reason he had stayed around was because he had the responsibility for taking care of Mom. He'd signed on to the job in 1955, after he finished college. She was his high school sweetheart and the light of his life ever since he'd laid eyes on her in 9th grade. She was his constant and faithful companion for almost 60 years, for better and for worse, bearing his children, keeping his house, and accompanying him on so many of his frequent travels across the United States and around the world. She provided companionship, material and moral support, and the fundamental foundation and reason for his being, and in return he provided the income necessary to make it all possible. And kids- me and my 2 younger brothers.

They'd made their last stand at a lovely, safe, well-appointed Senior Living facility in South Carolina, where the cost of living was cheap and the weather mostly hospitable. At first they lived together in an independent living apartment where he'd taken care of her as she descended incrementally into the fog of Alzheimer's. Eventually we had to move her up to the memory care unit, and until the last time he fell down when they had rolled him out on the gurney, he'd gone up there every day to sit on the couch and hold her hand, dozing through the endless re-runs of The Sound of Music, Singin' in the Rain, and My Fair Lady. Kiss her goodnight and whisper sweet nothings in her ear, hoping that somehow deep inside she still remembered who he was. Until one day she didn't remember anymore, and he let her go. In the three weeks time he spent in the hospital before he found that door with the Exit sign, he never mentioned Mom. I gently probed the subject a few times.

"Dad, have you seen Mom lately? How is she doing?"

Thinks for a minute, trying to recall.

"Yeah, um. She was.... busy."

"I'm taking care of her now, OK?" I say.

"OK. Yeah, um. She's in good hands."

He left her in my care. Me and the nurses at the Memory Care unit in South Carolina. Not that there was much left except for the shell. A vessel that had once contained a vibrant, joyful, loving young girl who fell in love and bore 3 children and traveled all over the world and lived as full a life as anyone could wish for. The bright flame of her spirit inside had long since gone, leaving only a dim spark, sputtering, a faint glowing ember with an occasional flicker of the gentle soul at the core of her being. So I cared for the vessel that had once contained my Mother and still held only a tiny trace of her. The body that had once been her home, now mostly vacant, was tied to this plane by the most tenuous of threads and a heart too noble to know when to stop.

It was impossible for me to abandon my home, family and job on the west coast and so I started commuting across the country every few weeks and hiring relief veterinarians. My husband lived on frozen pizza and dough-nuts while I was gone; he did a slightly better job at taking care of our dogs. My absence was hard on everyone. Within a short time after Dad's departure the staff at the Memory Care unit informed me that Mom was beginning to require a level of care above and beyond the qualifications of their staff, and that they would be moving her to the "Wellness Center" for skilled nursing. Well, I'd visited the "Wellness Center", and Dad was right. It simply was not an acceptable place for a person as fine and well-loved as my mother. Bare hallways echoing with the random wailing and ravings of dementia patients, terminal wrecks of human beings, minds gone, flesh remaining, lungs breathing, hearts beating, bowls and bladders still functioning- food in, excrement and urine out. Dispassionately tended by glazed and apathetic minimum wage nursing assistants and orderlies according to state mandated care protocols. Turn and clean every 4 hours. Meals served 3 times a day and thrown away 3 times a day. No. Not my Mom.

I'm certain Dad's restless spirit was the main reason I couldn't sleep or find peace until I just went and got her and brought her home to California with me. We hired contractors to do a quick remodel on our upstairs living quarters to turn it into a skilled nursing ward, packed her up and flew her across the country to live her last few months at "home" with loving family (me, Hank and the dogs) close by at all times. Not alone, not with strangers (a few of whom were as skilled as they were compassionate, others not so much.) With me. I knew her better than anyone else alive in the world. And I was the only one left who cared enough for her to make sure that every moment of her last days on earth would be comfortable, peaceful and full of love. And dignity. With her insurance we hired several home care nurses and I hovered over them like a tyrant, insisting on nothing less than 100% complete attentiveness, patience, gentleness and sensitivity. Hospice nurses came and went- I participated in every detail of her care. When the nurses' shifts were over I did the other 16 hours of the day myself, corralling my tired but faithful husband into helping when necessary. And it was increasingly necessary. Mom declined quickly. She mostly just wanted to sleep, so we let her sleep. I took care of the vessel, and kept her clean, comfortable, hydrated and nourished. I surrounded her with photos and mementos and treasures from her life. During her last week I "moved in" to the armchair next to her bed and rarely left her side. When I did step away I would feel anxious and in a hurry to return to her side, alert to any change or any hint she needed something or comfort I could provide. No doubt about it- the old man was possessing me most of the time, driving my obsession to be with her.

Sitting by her side, watching her breath, I escaped into fantasies of taking a long getaway when my vigil was over- rewarding myself with a hike or backpacking trip I'd always dreamed about doing someday- the Pacific Crest Trail or the Appalachian Trail, perhaps. I got on-line and read about the trails, trip reports, blogs. I ordered maps and books. I watched my Mother sleep away the last few months of her long rich life and though about doing all of the things that I had always dreamed about doing "someday when I get a chance" but had been putting off because I couldn't afford to take the time off to pursue them. I had to work and earn money, I had to go to school, study, and work to pay for my schooling, I had to support myself, my family and pay the mortgage, I had to take care of the dogs, my husband, my clinic, my co-workers, my patients and my clients..... everyone except me. Watching Mom breath I suddenly began to feel like time might be running out. Already I could feel the aches and pains of my accumulating years and the inevitable disassembling of this mortal flesh and blood. Hair thinning, joints stiffening, brain slowing, forgetting. No. I wouldn't follow Mom. I would not forget everything and become so helpless. Or at least not until I'd lived more. A LOT more!

Mom crossed over to the next world in August, eight months behind Dad. In my imagination I pictured Dad waiting for her impatiently from the other side and swooping down to claim her and scoop her up the instant she crossed over, escorting her to join him on the other side. I imagined a joyous reunion on that higher plane of existence, immortal souls free from the prisons of corrupted flesh and blood.

I took care of their remains, and their estate, and dealt with all of the Stuff they had left behind- worldly treasures only of value to them as mementos of the life they had lived and all the things they had seen and done. I took care of my brothers. I started hiking again and eventually went back to work. But every day I was haunted by reliving the events of the past year, wondering and worrying whether I should have done something differently. Obsessiveness took over. How might I have intervened earlier and gotten Dad the care he needed? How might I have taken an indefinite leave of absence from work and moved across the country to take care of them- how might I have paid the bills at home, taken care of the house, fed my husband, walked the dogs etc. Should I have moved Mom across the country when I did or let her stay in South Carolina even though it would have meant transferring her to the "Wellness Center"? Was she really any happier or more comfortable at our house? Everyone- my brothers, the hospice nurses & clergy, my counselor, my coworkers and even the staff at the Memory Care unit reassured me- there is no place like home, with family. But did Mom really ever know where she was? I constantly second guessed myself. I used to ask her if she knew where she was, and sometimes she would respond with a slight shake of her head or murmur, "no." I'd hug her and say "you're at home!" Smile. "The doctor finally said you could come home, and here you are!" Nod. I asked her if she remembered me, and she usually said yes. I believed her.

The moment Dad was gone I had begun worrying over the details of her care, waking up in the small hours of the night to check on her, turn her, adjust the sheets and pillows, and makes notes and orders for the nurses. I constantly questioned my decisions- was there more I could do, medicine I could give or not give. The waking up and obsessive second guessing of myself became habit- a familiar well worn mental rut that I hiked down every night, always with the same result or conclusion. She died. It wasn't easy. I think it was painless. Considering all of the dogs and cats I've euthanized over the past 25 years, I wasn't prepared for those last 72 hours. Usually my patients skip that part; it's over within a few seconds. Mom took longer to let go, and that was agonizing for me, but it was the only route over the pass. I was climbing it again and again every night when I left the West Coast for Vermont at the end of August. The Long Trail would change everything.

At a little past 5 in the morning in my tent at Tillotsen camp I suddenly woke up, about to explode, bowel-wise. I raced to the outhouse praying that it was not occupied by one of the five gentlemen staying in the cabin. Just imagine his shock when I burst in and plopped down on his lap! Ha! Surprise! Well, as Shrek says, better out than in! It seemed like everything I'd eaten in the past two days left on a fast train out of town. All I could think about was the parmesan cheese I'd added to my soup. Something was wrong with it. Don't ask me how I knew. The ghost of parmesan haunted my taste buds as I perched in the Stygian darkness on the outhouse throne.

Fully awake, cleaned up inside and out, I set about striking my tent and packing my gear. By dawn I was ready to hike.

Chapter 2

September 5, 2016

Day 3
Devils Gulch

I love this Trail! She is cruel and uncompromising as well as green and glorious. She gives as good as she gets. A proud Spirit- she pushes you to your limits, and then demands more. Those are her terms- take it or leave it. There's no easy way- climb, or go home. The rewards are commensurate with the punishment. The forest gives you unmatched peace and quiet and serenity. The moist greenery is a balm to parched souls. The bright arrays of mushrooms, the curling parchments of white and yellow birch bark scattered here and there, the patterns in the boulders and ancient exposed bedrock- all conspire to remove me to a world apart from the one in which I have been living. I stop thinking altogether about politics (so ugly), the war in Syria (so heart-breaking), and work issues (so never-ending). I focus on counting how many times I plant my trekking pole- 10 on the right, switch hands, 10 on the left, repeat. The meditation frees my mind from the usual obsessions and allows me to stay in the moment. The climbs are not so hard when you are simply taking one step at a time instead of thinking about how high and distant is the summit.

The first challenge of the day was finding the trail out of Tillotsen camp. You might laugh, but it was harder than you'd think. I had come into camp from the Northwest, that was easy. From Tillotsen Camp the Long Trail southbound actually departed by backtracking in a northwest direction for short while. The confusion

came about because an access trail came in from the east and terminated at the cabin, and it was logical to assume this spur was the continuation of the Long Trail. Except that it didn't have white blazes and was clearly marked "Frank Post Trail." I stumbled around for 20 minutes before realizing that I was indeed supposed to be heading out of town the same direction I'd come in from, just on a slightly different path. Adding to the confusion was a network of user created trails from the cabin to the outhouse, the water source and all around the interesting features of the area. I sure didn't want to end up at the outhouse again. In the end I simply followed Lyssa and we got lucky. (It wasn't the first time I'd adopted that strategy; Lyssa had a nose for navigation.)

On the morning of day 3 we climbed up Belvedere Peak. It was steep and rugged, of course. The men from the cabin burned past me before long, marching like commandos on a mission in the jungle. They were grunting. Machines, I thought. Later as I sat

and wrote my journal I couldn't remember the climb at all- I knew when I was doing the climb it felt endless and exhausting- but all I could remember was the view from the top and the cup of hot coffee I brewed when I was up there and how good I felt after that. Onward. Going down Belvedere, we started to meet a lot of people on the trail, I guess because it was Labor Day Weekend. For the first time I had to put Lyssa on leash. Lyssa is big and can be intimidating sometimes. Also the forest at lower elevations is full of chipmunks which have an annoying habit of sounding off with an alarm chirp just as we are passing by, and Lyssa couldn't help but pounce on them. They were always too smart for her, and were long gone by the time she pounced or crashed off into the bush after them, but I was afraid she'd get hurt or rip up her saddle bags.

As the conifer forest gave way to broad-leafs, the trail became more open and congenial. Lots of inviting creeks and waterways beckoned for drinking and cooling off. I relaxed and dallied a bit, refreshing myself in a beautiful brook running alongside the trail. My stomach was behaving, we were going downhill on an easy trail with no rocks, and my normal good spirits began to revive and re-emerge. When we crossed highway 118, and the scene changes into a middle landscape of abandoned farmland. It's a dramatic switch from yesterday's hellish climb up the bruising vertical chaos of boulders and brush. The land south of 118 must have been cultivated farmland at one time because the trees are all young growths of slender beech and maple, and there are lines of tumbled down rock walls everywhere. Was it too cold and rugged for the farmer to make it? I wonder. Perhaps the farmers' children inherited the land and were happy to sell it to land grabbing conservationists who wanted to create a permanent right of way for the Long Trail. The old walls were beautiful works of art, covered with thick moss and lichen, drawing random lines through the forest. I thought about all the work it took to build them by hand, one stone at a time, perhaps tossed by the farmer as he turned the rocky soil to plant a crop. We were climbing up again, but the trail was gentle and gradual, a walk in the park compared to the rocky sluice-way we confronted just yesterday. Tired and moving at a slow pace, we eventually we reached the Ritterbush Lookout, just above (what else?) Ritterbush Pond. I rested a bit, and read about Devil's Gulch.

The entrance to Devils Gulch

From the guidebook: Devil's Gulch is "the challenging route along the floor of the gulch among jumbled boulders." That's all it says. No explanation of the somewhat alarming satanic reference. I might not have thought twice about diving right in except that I had learned to be a little bit wary of the book's tendency to understate things. Wasn't that a New England thing, understate-

Lyssa found her own way up out of Devils Gulch

ment? Concerning Haystack the book commented simply "drop very steeply to a brook." So far Lyssa and Tina had been amazing in their ability to scramble up and down everything the Trail had thrown at us. But Lyssa had trouble squeezing through tight spots. I can take her packs off of her if necessary, but I can't lift her up a vertical rock face. Surely someone would have told me if the gulch was impossible for dogs, I thought. There was only one way to find out.

Devil's Gulch was fun: an agility course designed by our playful Trail Spirit just for sport! I relieved Lyssa of her pack and let her find her own way through the boulders. She was amazing at figuring out how to get up and around and over the obstacles, and it was a joy to watch her work. Tina is amazing too. She should have been a circus dog. Tina can do 5.4 free climbs with no problem. Up or down, doesn't matter. Nobody ever believes me when I say this, but it's the truth! I appreciate my trail companions more and more. They are smart, strong, nimble, sure-footed, loyal and faithful friends. They know what we are doing- we are traveling this Trail. They are with me all the time, every day, every step, on the Trail. The strength of our bond, their devotion to me and my deep appreciation of them-- these are also gifts from the Trail. I am grateful.

After Devil's Gulch we took a break at Spruce Ledge Camp. It's a bit off the trail, but boasts a nice place to sit with a good view. There is a great stream crossing right where you turn off the Long Trail to go up to the shelter. It would have been a lovely spot to spend the night and I surely would have benefited from a nice long rest. But there were some day hikers wandering in and out, and for some reason Tina had decided to bark at them. So after a quick snack I pressed on, with the hope that Bowen Mountain might offer a good place to spend the night, and maybe a view. I did not fill up the water bags at the stream, gambling that we'd come across a source on the way up Bowen Mountain. It seemed like a reasonable gamble- the creeks and waterholes had been plentiful all day.

The hike up to Bowen was dry. Even though we were only a few days away from the Canadian border we had crossed into a slightly less alpine ecosystem. More southern and a little less watery. I kicked myself. I'd taken the chance on finding water because I was tired and didn't want to deal with extra weight while walking up Bowen Mountain. Now we were stuck with the prospect of camping without any water at all or continuing on into the unknown, possibly in the dark. When would I ever learn? When we reached the summit where the trail crosses the shoulder of Bowen Mountain I stopped to study the map- and the clock. We were in luck. One mile ahead was a low spot, where the trail crossed numerous tributaries of Basin Brook. We could find water and a place to camp. From the summit I sent a quick text update to Hank, knowing that I probably would not have service down in the lowland.

We camp well away from the trail near a small brook, a tributary of Basin Brook, somewhere between Bowen and Butternut Mountains.The forest is canopy is thick, and the undergrowth is lush. Because we are low in a basin, surrounded by hills the sun sets early and it gets dark early. The water murmurs a lullaby; we're in a good, safe place and we're on schedule, going strong. I drift off into a deep relaxed sleep.

September 6, 2016

Day 4
Laraway Mountain

Sometimes you find strength in unexpected places. Long after that peaceful night at Basin Brook I had good reason to think of a lesson learned there, courtesy of my friendly hostess Long Trail Spirit.

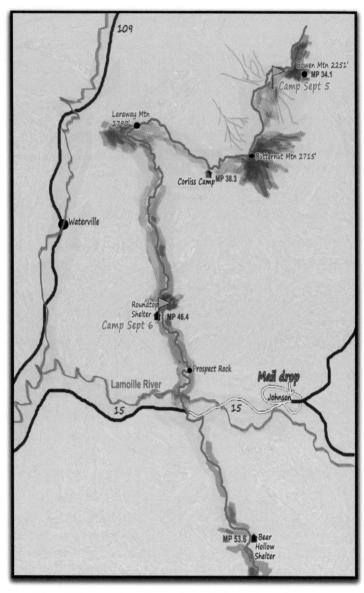

Map 3: Bowen Mtn, Roundtop Shelter, the Johnson side-trip and Bear Hollow Shelter on the way up Whiteface.

I'm normally a "glass half full" kind of person, basically optimistic and able to find a silver lining in any situation. But sometimes a lot of bad things happen at once and my defenses get overwhelmed. A few months after I got home from Vermont I had such a day. I got unfriended for the first time on Facebook. I woke up to find a tick glommed on to my belly, causing a nasty infected looking lump. The neighbor who owns the 140 acre parcel next to us announced his intention to do a timber harvest, which means we'll have chainsaws, trucks, and bulldozers invading this summer. My car was in the shop with a defective catalytic converter. I had a bad day at work. To top it all off there was a pathological liar sitting in the White House gleefully dismantling the constitutional fabric of our democratic society. I had to think awhile to come up with a reason to not give in to despair, but then I remembered, "at least I don't live in Oroville."

Oroville and surrounding towns are located in the Feather River Valley, downstream from the world's tallest dam. The Oroville Dam was built in 1968 and Lake Oroville is a crucial component of the water supply system for the whole Central Valley of California. For several years the lake levels have been dangerously low, due to years of drought and poor snow-pack. But the winter of 2016 we had torrential rains, warm rains which worked to melt the snow-pack that had accumulated from a series of earlier, colder storms, and the Lake Oroville was full. So full that the Department of Water Resources had begun releasing water over the main spillway, which is a concrete chute adjacent to the dam itself. All was fine and dandy until someone noticed a hole forming in the concrete chute. The Department of Water Resources (DWR) turned off the water so that they could inspect the damage. "Might be trouble," they concluded, "but there's always the back-up emergency spillway as a failsafe in case we need it." No danger, they said. And they turned the water back on but at a reduced rate of flow so that the hole wouldn't get too much of a pounding.

Meanwhile it rained a lot more up in the mountains and Lake Oroville continued to rise. DWR officials cleared the brush away from the outflow of the emergency spillway, which had never been used. Early Saturday morning the Lake topped out and water began to trickle over the concrete lip at the top of the emergency spillway and down the earthen slope. Just as planned. The trickle turned into a torrent as more and more water flowed into the Lake, fed by high altitude snow fields melting in unseasonably warm temperatures. At about 2:30 in the afternoon somebody noticed that one of the channels in the face of the emergency spillway, which had eroded rapidly and severely under the vast torrent of water pouring down, had reached the concrete lip and looked to be undermining it. Assessment: the emergency spillway could collapse any minute, causing uncontrolled release of flood waters into the Feather River. Oroville and the whole Feather River Valley could be under water in an hour or two. Emergency mandatory evacuation orders were given and 180,000 people ran for their lives. In case you missed it on the news and were watching the Grammy awards, or following the continuing saga of "what did the President know and when did he know it," the emergency spillway did not fail. They increased the flow in the main spillway, which luckily did not fail either despite the huge gaping hole in the concrete. The Lake level dropped and a whole army of helicopters came and dropped rocks into the eroded channels. California dodged the bullet, this time.

The point of all this is as follows: a tick bite, an unfriending, a timber harvest, a car repair, an angry client and a political downturn, even when added up all together, do not equal a catastrophic flood washing away your home and everything you hold dear. Which did not happen, fortunately. But it could have. Things could have been much worse than they are.

When things seem bad, when bad things are stacking up and conspiring against you look at the Big Picture. Take a deep breath and think. Keep yourself safe. Make a plan and then creep towards it. Change the things you can and accept the rest. Things will get better. This is a Gift of the Trail- a bit of wisdom to remember and use when needed. It came to me in Basin Brook, very early in the morning of Day 4. The night was still as dark as a dungeon. No starlight, no moonlight, nothing penetrated. We were all sleeping soundly, lulled by the nearby happy gurgle of the brook. After 3 long days of hiking, Lyssa had given up on night time guard duty, and was sleeping soundly through the night.

I woke up suddenly in the darkness with an urgent telegram from deep within: "S**t Happening- Gotta Go Now!" I felt around for my shoes. I didn't have time to spare, but I couldn't go staggering off into the brush barefoot and risk a bruise, laceration or worse. My feet had to stay strong and whole, or the trip was toast. I always keep my shoes close by in the same spot at night so I can find them in the dark. That's one of those hard-earned little tips that can make a big difference in how much you enjoy your trip. It paid off. Shoes on, forget the socks, be careful of the laces. I grabbed my toilet kit, my water bottle, my jacket and my solar charged flashlight and made a mad dash across the brook. (Going to the other side of the brook just seemed like a good idea; don't ask me why.) It wasn't the thickest brush I've ever gone crashing through, but there were plenty of branches, logs, rocks, dips and soft muddy holes to make it challenging. I thrashed my way as far from the brook as I could go and at the last second dropped trousers and assumed the position. My bowels exploded in a jet of gas and fluid, and then suddenly things got worse. The solar flashlight started blinking and 10 seconds later blinked out. Leaving me squatting in absolute and utter black darkness.

I couldn't move. For one thing, my ankles were basically tied together because my woolen sleeping tights were dropped around them. I was also hovering an inch away from a puddle of poo and the last thing I wanted to do was touch it or God Forbid fall in it. I felt a little off balance with no light to orient myself to objects around me. Pro Tip: When pooping in the woods it's a good idea to situate yourself next to a handy log, rock or sapling in order to steady yourself and assist in rising from the low crouch. But now I wasn't sure what was around me. OK, no hurry, I told myself. First, finish the job at hand. Find the toilet kit, and then figure out how to get back to the tent and my gear. Absolutely blind, I cautiously felt around until I found my kit. Found the soap, the rag, the water jug and didn't spill it. Cleaned up, remembering where I put everything because I can't loose anything- especially Tina's pills and all my first aid supplies- and carefully stood up. Then I remembered that my phone was in my jacket pocket and I could use it as a flashlight! I was saved! I fumbled for the phone, happily finding it, and carefully- not dropping it- pushed home button. The low battery icon appeared briefly and faded. The phone was dead. I had forgotten to put it in airplane mode last night, and because there was no signal in the basin it had roamed all night long. I had fallen asleep trying to send a check- in text message to Hank. (Sometimes if I leave it on for awhile a stray signal will get through and deliver the message. Or not.) But the text had failed to send, and now everything was dead. Dead phone, dead solar charger. I was stuck in thick brush, in pitch black darkness, away from my gear. I took a deep breath and thought for a few minutes. The main thing was not to get in real trouble by getting myself hurt. It wasn't like I could call for help with a dead phone and no signal. And I was far enough away from the main trail that it would be tough to find me. I imagined Lyssa and Tina flagging down passersby and leading them to my dessicated remains. It wasn't unheard of for a careless hiker to wander off the trail for a bathroom break and end up totally lost- and dead! If necessary I could just stay put until it was light enough to see. How long would that be? Hours, I guessed. It was too chilly to sit and wait. I needed to move if I could. Carefully.

It would be easy to trip and fall; branches, logs, holes, mud pits and rocks were all around. I could walk into a

52

branch and lacerate myself, knock myself out or loose an eye. Or trip over my shoelaces. "I'm okay," I thought. "Things could be worse- it could be raining!" How nice it was not to be soaking wet in addition to being lost in the brush in absolute blackness with my pants down and uncontrollable diarrhea! And even better- at least I had made it out of the sleeping bag before exploding! Look on the bright side. I tied my shoelaces and gathered my gear, gripping it firmly in one hand. With the other hand I felt the ground in front of me, felt for any branches in my way. Clear. Take one step. Which way do I go? The forest was dead silent, like a tomb, except for.... the brook! I could hear gurgling, faintly. I had to go back to the brook and cross it, and find my tent. The Voice of Dad spoke in my brain: "If you can't run, walk. And if you can't walk, crawl." This was a time for crawling.

On hands and knees I slowly inched my way towards the sound of the brook, carefully feeling my way over across and through every obstacle in my path until at last I was on the edge of the brook. Still feeling my way, I managed to climb down the bank and across the water. When I was about 5 feet from my tent I saw it- a faint blob, ever so slightly less dark than the surrounding dark. I gratefully slipped back into my cozy sleeping bag, thought about the trail ahead, and waited for the dawn.

Things could always be worse. I don't live in Oroville and didn't have to evacuate suddenly in the face of a potential catastrophic flood. Some bad things had happened and I was feeling pretty stressed out, but then I remembered the lesson of Basin Brook: Hold on to what you have. Be careful. Stay safe. Don't fall in shit. Crawl if you have to. Dawn comes.

Day 4 promised to be fairly pleasant. I was aiming for Roundtop Shelter, 11 miles ahead. The biggest climb of the day was Laraway Mountain with a reasonable looking graded ascent. Not like Haystack. I was well-rested and my pack felt noticeably lighter. My phone was dead and so was my flashlight, but I survived the early morning reprise of Revenge of the Killer Parmesan, and my bowels were finally settling down for real. Hank would be worried but I figured that I might be able to get a little charge out of my solar panel if I paid more attention to positioning it to face the sun. When I hike on the West Coast all I have to do is lash the panel to the top of my pack and I have no problem collecting enough of a current to fully charge up the phone every night. Hiking under the thick canopy of the Vermont forest is a different story. But on September 6 there was not a single cloud in the sky and the forest promised to be much more open and brightly lit than it had been further north. I celebrated my health and continuing good progress with a cup of hot coffee on Butternut Mountain.

Corliss Camp boasted such an adorable little cabin for a shelter that I regretted not being able to stay at it. I would like to live in a little cabin like that, I thought. Life would have to be simple and stress-free in such a tiny home. It seemed so inviting with it's little front porch and windows, especially the artistic setting of the window in the front door. I loved the mossy roof and dappled sunlight playing over everything. It was perfect. It would be all I needed. I could retire and run away and live in a tiny cabin in the woods, in Vermont. Off the grid... or was it?

Corliss Cabin

54

Obsessively I checked my phone and was surprised when the power came on! There was no cell service, so I took a photo of Corliss cabin as a reminder that there is a place like this in the world for me and all I have to do is find it.

At Corliss the Long Trail South takes an abrupt turn to the North west, and follows a crooked dog-legged detour up and over Laraway Mountain. The trail architects must have had good reasons for throwing in an extra 3 miles and 1,000 feet of strenuous climbing up and down, but I can only speculate as to what those reasons may have been. Most likely it was simply because the view from Laraway Mountain was breathtakingly beautiful. Heaven could not be more heavenly than this sunny ledge in the sky overlooking the lovely green pastoral Lamoille River Valley. It was gorgeous. And sunny. I rested while my phone climbed to a hefty 4% charge and I then called Hank. His fussiness and dismay about the failure in communications could not diminish my bliss. I was in heaven- hiking the Long Trail in Vermont! Finally, after all the months of planning and preparing, I was here. This was where I wanted to be. Looking at this view. It was idyllic. Even the weather was perfect. I was where I was supposed to be.

At 2,790' Laraway summit is high enough to be spruce covered, and once again we faced a strenuous descent down eroded bedrock gullies to reach the balmier open hardwood forests below. Five rambling rural roller-coaster miles through abandoned upstate Vermont farmland later I arrived at Roundtop Shelter, situated on a wooded knoll with a nice view of the sunset. With only one other occupant, a congenial young East Indian man named Seleem, there was plenty of room in the lean-to. I gave in to laziness and opted to set up my sleeping bag in the clean sturdy looking shelter instead of setting up my tent nearby. At dusk the girls and I settled in for a nice long restful night. No sooner had we dozed off when two more hikers arrived, south-bounders, huffing and puffing up the hill with huge overloaded packs. In short order they occupied the picnic table and the remaining space in the lean-to, scattering gear hither and yon, and proceeded to cook up a giant pot of macaroni and cheese. It smelled delicious. They were section hikers, just out for a few days, and more interested in comfort than in lightening their loads. They were kindly tolerant of my dogs and I was kindly tolerant of their disturbance, although I began to regret not having camped further down the trail.

It was a restless night. Unbeknown to me until that night, an inflated air mattress on a raised wooden floor creates a kind of resonant amplifier of sound, especially the rustling sound of nylon sleeping bags. Every time anyone moved the sound of rustling nylon filled the lean-to. I toss and turn a lot. My hips get stiff from lying on my side, and I roll on my back. But I can't sleep on my back and so I roll onto the other side. I sleep best on my stomach, but that makes my back hurt. So around and round I go. Every time I rolled over the dogs got up and re-adjusted themselves. Acutely conscious of trying not to disturb my shelter-mates I tried extra hard to relax, but the harder I tried to hold still, the more I wanted to toss and turn. It didn't help that I was feeling extremely anxious about the next day when I was scheduled to pick up my first mail drop. It was in the town of Johnson 2.8 miles east of the trail on highway 15. Would I be able to hitch a ride? What if I had to walk all of the way because no one picked me up? Could I keep the dogs safe on a busy two lane highway? What if I got picked up by a psychopath? What if my supply box was missing? What if I couldn't find the post office? How would I be able to recharge my phone and my solar panel battery? What if I couldn't take the dogs into the post office? Would it be safe to leave the dogs outside the grocery store so I could do some shopping? Was I keeping everyone awake by tossing and turning again?

At the first hint of light I crept out of bed and started the chore of collecting and stowing my gear, feeding the girls and preparing for the day's adventures. Seleem was up early too, doing yoga, and we headed down the trail together before the macaroni men emerged from their sleeping bags. It was good to be moving.

Chapter 3

September 7, 2016

Day 5
Johnson

Johnson will be the first of three resupply detours, which means I am almost 1/4 finished with my trip- that is to say 1/4 done time-wise, but certainly not in terms of distance. Johnson is about 55 miles south of the Northern terminus- barely 1/5 of the way. Obviously I will have to make up some mileage further south where the trail is allegedly much "flatter" and "smoother". All the north-bound hikers use those words. They sound beautiful. But to get to Johnson, Lyssa and Tina and I have to get from the Highway 15/ LT trail intersection to the Johnson Post Office, which is a 2.3 mile tromp down a busy 2-lane highway. I've never hitch-hiked before. I've been assured that Vermonters are very generous and accustomed to picking up Long Trail hikers in these parts, but what about hikers with giant German Shepherds? At least with Lyssa along I won't have to worry about getting picked up by a rapist or a robber. Unless he has a gun. If he tries to shoot my dog he will have to shoot me first. I am so stressed out by the prospect of hitchhiking to Johnson I hurry down the trail to the highway crossing in record time, leaving Seleem to enjoy a morning meditation on Prospect Rock.

Turns out it's hard to hitch a ride when you're traveling with an 85 pound German Shepherd. Milk trucks, utility trucks, over-sized pick-up trucks, giant SUVs, conservation minded liberals in hybrid economy cars, even Volkswagen buses- all whiz by me as if I am invisible. They don't even slow down. Not even with Lyssa sitting obediently and elegantly by my side. Out on the road the sun is so bright I must dig out my sunglasses for the first time since I started walking. The pavement is hot and the dogs are thirsty already at 9 in the morning. Finally a van pulls over and I jog gratefully up to it. Surprise- in the passenger seat is Seleem! He spotted me by the side of the road and begged his driver to pick me up! It strikes me as remarkable and wryly funny that Seleem, who is young, male and has brown skin, had no trouble getting a ride, whereas I, a mature Caucasian female with 2 beautiful well-mannered dogs, could not. There is a lesson there somewhere, but I'll be darned if I can figure it out. Almost everyone I meet admires my dogs- they take photos of Lyssa looking beautiful and noble with her packs- but they don't want to let us get in their cars. Beats me.

The van driver dropped us off at the Johnson shopping center, by the post office and grocery store. The postmaster wouldn't let the dogs into the post office, so I tied them outside the door with my pack and a bowl of water, and watched them anxiously through the window while I waited at the counter to claim my re-supply box. The hustle and bustle of this tiny north country New England town was overwhelming. The dogs laid down and watched serenely as people and cars paraded by. I had so much to do before I could head back to the trail, but all I could think about was whether I would be able to get a ride back. Everyone was friendly and loved the dogs. But would they give us a ride? I didn't know. Seleem got his box and started sorting through it, and I trusted him to watch the girls while I dashed into the grocery store and bought a few snacks. I didn't really need a whole lot- some fresh fruit, a pastry and some ginger ale hit the spot. I plugged my phone into an outlet near the door of the Post Office where I could keep an eye on it. All of the details of reorganizing, resorting, repacking and recharging frazzled my nerves and made my head spin. On top of it all I needed to call Hank and check in so that he would stop worrying, but there was no privacy or comfortable place to sit out there in front of the Post Office.

It seemed to take forever to sort through my box and get everything stowed away. I stuffed five days worth of garbage into the trash at the post office. Then I sorted out a few items of gear that I was not using- including my sadly useless solar panel, some dirty socks, and Lyssa's sturdy leather leash which I replaced with a lightweight piece of parachute cord- and I shipped it all back to Hank. Seleem wandered off to find the town library so he could shop for new boots and Skype his girlfriend. The sun was hot on the pavement- I wanted only to get back to the shady forest. Finally I was ready. Miraculously I remembered my phone! It wasn't fully recharged, but I couldn't wait another moment. Lyssa was less than thrilled when I put her pack on her, now heavily laden with six days worth of dog food. My pack felt monstrously heavy too. A woman took our picture. We posed cheerfully, and then asked her for a ride to the trail head. She was headed the other way. Damn.

We walk to the edge of town and I stick out my thumb. But the same thing happens on the way out of town- nobody stops, nobody even slows down. Traffic thunders by us- so many trucks in this quiet country town. The pavement is hot and sharp on the dogs' feet and the shoulder of the highway is a rough and narrow strip of gravel, weeds and trash. I can tell they are not enjoying this any more than I am. There is a gas station/ convenience store on the other side of the highway and I decide to try my luck there. Maybe I can call a taxi! A woman is sitting in the parking lot in a huge black pick-up truck, eating a snack from the store. I

*swallow my pride and ask her if by any chance she is head-
ing west. She looks at Lyssa and shakes her head. I explain
that my dogs' feet are getting burned on the pavement we
only need to go two miles and I'd be glad to ride in the back
with them. She can't refuse the dogs. Before she can change
her mind I somehow lift Lyssa, saddle bags and all, into the
bed of the truck, and then Tina and I climb in. I give my
driver $20 at the trail-head in hopes she might be more
inclined to pick up hikers with dogs in the future.*

*We've made it- our first maildrop! It was every bit as much
of an ordeal as Haystack; given a choice, I'd have climbed
Haystack again. I'm ecstatic to be back on the trail and
back in the quiet cool forest. I realize that the trail feels like
home, even though I'm moving all of the time. Every step is
home. Every step is the same, and I am always in the same
place- one step further than I was before, and one step
away from where I will be next. I am always in that place
of being one step ahead and one step behind, and always in
the same place, which is on the Trail. Maybe this is what it
means to be in the moment, I don't know. It feels good and
my tension of the last few hours subsides. Even though we
will soon face an intimidating ascent of Whiteface Mountain, there is no place I would rather be than here on the
Long Trail.*

Leaving Johnson, it wasn't easy to find the trail again. The
route is not well marked and there is a confusing jum-
ble of dirt roads, logging roads and walking paths to be
navigated. I consulted the guide book and the gps repeatedly, asked (generally clueless) passersby for directions
and only made a few wrong turns. By mid-afternoon we
were back on real trail, out of the logging area, and in the
forest. Presently we arrived at Bear Hollow Shelter, and
much to our surprise we were greeted by the Macaroni
brothers! They had bypassed the temptations of civilization in Johnson, and having had as much difficulty as I did
in navigating the tangled track south of Highway 15, they

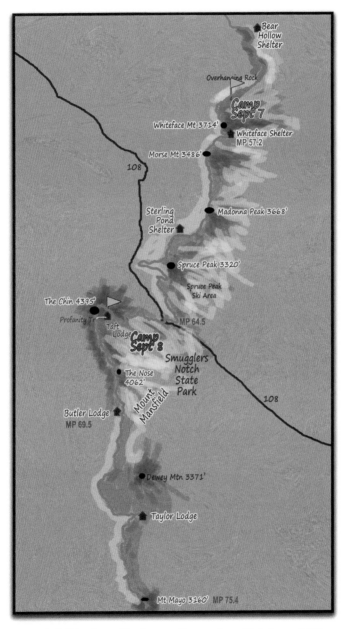

Bear
Hollow
Shelter

Overhanging Rock

Camp
Sept 7

Whiteface Mt 3714'
Whiteface Shelter
MP 57.2

Morse Mt 3486'

108

Sterling
Pond
Shelter

Madonna Peak 3668'

Spruce Peak 3320'

Spruce Peak
Ski Area

The Chin 4395'

MP 64.5

Profanity Tr

Taft
Lodge

Camp
Sept 8

Smugglers
Notch
State
Park

The Nose
4062'

108

Mount
Mansfield

Butler Lodge
MP 69.5

Dewey Mtn 3371'

Taylor Lodge

Mt Mayo 3160' MP 75.4

Map 4: Whiteface, Madonna, Smugglers Notch, and Mt Mansfield.

61

were ready to call it a day. I wanted more miles. We'd only come 7.2 trail miles that day and my quota was supposed to be 10. Tina, evidently, did not care. She planted herself in the middle of the picnic table, conveniently in position for the boys to be able to rub her belly in case they were so inclined. They were. I relaxed and opened the Guide Book.

The summit of Whiteface Mountain towers 3,200 feet above the Lamoille River Valley and the town of Johnson. On the map the elevation profile is as steep as any of the major steep mountains on the Long Trail, and the net gain for the climb is greater than the ascent of Mt Mansfield. Reaching Bear Hollow Shelter was a good start, but it was still 3 miles to the summit with the steepest sections yet to come. Consulting the book I noticed a stream close by the trail about 2 miles up towards summit, just before the contour lines started getting really close together. I could camp there and be in a good position to tackle the steep final ascent of Whiteface in the morning, when I was fresh. I'd heard it was pretty brutal. One hiker I met told me he'd come down Whiteface during a thunderstorm, slipping and sliding on the steep rocks so much that he was certain he was going to fall and break a leg, or worse. The forecast was calling for a chance of rain the next day. I did not want to climb Whiteface in the rain. It would be a challenge even on a perfect day, and I had a full pack, heavier than ever. Once again driven by anxiety about the challenge ahead, I pushed on.

I hadn't gone very far when I realized something was missing. I only had one dog. For the first time ever in her life, Tina had not followed me when I walked down the trail. That little traitor! She had stayed with the Macaroni Men! What a rat! Sold out for a piece of Wisconsin cheddar! I backtracked towards Bear Hollow and spotted my little dog sitting in the middle of the trail about 50 yards from the lean-to. Forlornly. I called her. She sat there. Stubborn. I turned and walked ahead down the trail a ways. Looked back. She was still sitting there. Grumbling,

I walked down to her and picked her up. Lugged her up the trail a good ways. After awhile I put her down. She sat where I put her and watched me walk on up the path. I continued. The next time I turned around she was still sitting in the trail but had moved up my direction. What if she decided to turn around and

Tina found the Bear Hollow Shelter very much to her liking

go back to Bear Hollow? She had to know I would go back for her. This was a test of wills! Pulling out a leash, I went back and attached my poor pitiful little companion to me. After a few tugs she gave in, and before long she was in front of me, tripping along with her usual springy step. Eventually I let her off the leash, and she stayed with me, no problem. But that night I gave her a good helping of tuna with an extra large scoop of kibbles. Just wanted to lighten the load, of course.

After an hour or so of slow and steady climbing we

Mount Mansfield Skyline

passed Overhanging Rock, and then I began to notice a few spruce trees scattered here and there among the birches and maples, as sure sign that we were reaching higher elevation. The spruces began thickening and soon I heard the welcome gurgling of a brook paralleling the trail on our left. We hopped off the trail and found a cozy level spot near the brook, and made ourselves at home for the night.

Resting in the quiet forest, I let my mind wander. There was no cell signal. It was just me and two dogs in the wilderness, high on the shoulder of Whiteface Mountain. I was neither alone, nor lonely.

Some things just have an impact on you whether you like it or not. Taking care of Mom for the last months of her life had an impact on me whether she wanted it to or not. And she did not. She always adamantly did not want to be a burden, or even a minor nuisance. She didn't want to hinder, ever, only to be of help. That was her nature. All of our lives she promised us that she would never be a burden on us. We would be free to come and go and pursue our own dreams, lives and ambitions and she would never make any demands on us or get in our way. Where did my folks get this idea, that we would not want to help them if they needed it? That our lives were somehow more important than theirs, or that we would expect them to take care of themselves even if they were crippled or feeble or handicapped. Didn't we owe it to them? They brought us into the world and took care of us for so many years- didn't we owe them something? They said no. Had they resented taking care of their parents when they were old? Where did they get the idea that I would not want to help them if they needed help. Was there anyone else more appropriate for the job? Did they expect that they would be able to fend for themselves until the bitter end? It must have been something cultural that they picked up by growing up when they did- a social value that decreed that children should not be indebted to their parents. I suspect that if indeed this was a social value of their generation it was a uniquely American value. In other cultures and in other eras parents and grandparents all lived together with children in extended family units. Having children was part of the retirement plan. Old people weren't warehoused in nursing homes in most parts of the world. Instead they lived with their children. They continued to contribute what they could to the household but the children were responsible for their care. I thought it wasn't a bad idea- it would give the children a chance to learn about aging. In our culture we worship youth. Aging is disparaged and disrespected. Old people are shuttered away in nursing homes, where unspeakable things happen. Smelly undignified things happen. As if by hiding and sequestering our elders we can pretend it won't happen to us. Nobody wants to "end up" in a nursing home, slurping and shuffling and wearing diapers. Not happening, right. Hello? Old age and dementia creep up on you. You don't have a choice.

In the dark small hours of the night I thought about that stuff. Aging. The pitfalls thereof. It felt like dodging bullets, only the bullets were coming faster and thicker. I was exercising regularly, staying active, eating right, avoiding carcinogens, driving defensively- check. Funding the IRA and the 401k- check. But in the words of Hank Williams, "no matter how we struggle and strive, we never get out of this world alive." If my parents couldn't win in the battle against mortality, what hope did I have? I had to have a plan. There had to be a good answer to this dilemma- a way to fight time. I wanted to live forever, but barring that, at least for as long as I could. I took care of Mom, but who would take care of me? Maybe that's what kept me awake at night. I was still obsessing in this vein that night on Whiteface Mountain.

Since Mom was so determined never to be a burden or an imposition I had to wait until she was quite helpless and fairly oblivious to her surroundings to be able to bring her into my home where I could take care of her properly. In the end we could say that she achieved her wishes and

I achieved my wish to spend some time with her before she left, and assured that her last few months were spent in love and comfort.

Not that it wasn't a sacrifice: it was. We gave up half our house and I gave up almost all of my freedom and mobility. I gave up hiking, I gave up trips to the mountains, I cut back on work as much as I could and gave up much of our income, I gave up sleeping more than 2 hours at a time. It was worth it for the peace of mind of knowing she was always clean, comfortable and in the company of people who loved and appreciated her. But I knew that when it was over I would take some time for myself. I would pursue a dream of my own for awhile.

The fantasy of being completely free of my responsibilities and obligations often occupied my thoughts during the hours and days and weeks I sat by Mom's bedside. I felt that she was supportive of my dreams- she had always been supportive of my dreams, whatever they were, however crazy and ill-conceived. That's just how she was. Supportive and encouraging, even if it was a bad idea! She didn't judge, only said "ooh, that sounds like fun!" I communed with her sleeping body and told her about my idea for a great adventure, sometimes out loud but mostly silently, in that foggy mystical place where dying people go when they are in between this world and the next.

Now I was on the adventure and I wished I could share it with her. She would have loved it! Mom was my first hiking partner and was largely responsible for my life-long fascination with nature, wildlife and the forest. I had barely started walking when she took me to Mount Airy Forest to play in the meadow and explore the edges of the woods, full of deer, squirrels, chipmunks and birds. She told me that the song of the cardinal was him calling to me: "Shirley Shirley Shirley,"- and I believed it to be true. Calling me outside, calling me into the woods. In the fall we walked on the trails kicking the colorful falling leaves-flaming red oak and vibrant yellow maples, collecting the prettiest ones to bring home and press them flat in wax paper and admire. We played in the snow, built snow men, and snow forts, skated on the pond, and if we were lucky we'd go tobogganing. In the spring we'd go find the first flowers to bloom and admire the ice on the branches and blossoms after a late season storm. If there were gaps in my memories of all these things, there were all of the hundreds of photos Dad had taken to fill in the missing pieces and assure me that it had all been real. They took us camping and canoeing, and every summer there were many days spent on the beach, digging in the sand and playing in the surf. We were always outside, always on the go. She and Dad were surely close by that night by the brook in the forest on Whiteface Mountain.

September 8, 2016

Day 6
Whiteface, Smuggler's Notch

My memory of the early morning climb up Whiteface peak is already blurry and dreamlike. I had camped right at the forest transition zone, where the open hardwoods give way to spruces. As you ascend in elevation the thick conifers close in around you and the forest darkens. The trail steepens and suddenly becomes serious and intimidating, with sections of nearly vertical rock faces. At first these sections are only two to four feet tall, just a tall step. Then they become more like small rock-climbing ascents, where you have to stop and look for toe holds and hand-holds, and plan your route of attack. Eventually I put my pole away so that I can have both hands free for climbing. Several times I take my pack off and toss it up to a ledge overhead. The dogs are amazing, and encourage me to keep coming up behind them. I proceed very carefully, focusing on every foothold and handhold, staying safe and uninjured.

The summit is a bit of bare rock closed in by spruce trees. If I were 20 feet tall instead of a mere 5' 8, the view would probably be stunning. I continue on towards the Whiteface Shelter where I have promised myself a cup of hot coffee and a rest. It's only a half mile down to the shelter, which normally would be a 15 or 20 minute walk, but it took a good 45 minutes of focused and careful down-climbing.

Descending steep slippery rock faces is just as challenging as climbing up them, and a lot riskier for falling and getting injured. Sometimes it's easier to turn around and climb down backwards so that you can use your toes instead of your heels, but then its hard to see where the toeholds are. I like to reach ahead with my pole and find a secure spot to plant the tip, and then use it as a third leg while I hop down the face, hopefully to a solid landing spot. Luckily I have strong knees. When we hiked the John Muir Trail I learned to truly appreciate my sturdy knees and ligaments. Some less fortunate people have to ride a mule in order to get themselves into the back country, but I have my own mules in my knees. I named them Roy and Dale. On really long hikes sometimes I even talked to them: "Yee-haw, up you go Roy. That's the way to do it. Your turn Dale. Get along, up you go." They are reliable. It's good to appreciate your parts. Don't ever take knees for granted. Advice from the Mountain.

So far I had been lucky and the forecasted rain had not materialized. I made it safely over Whiteface without having to deal with the added challenge of wet rocks and transient streams of water coursing down the eroded gullies. The Whiteface Shelter was a welcome sight. It was only 9:30 in the morning, but it has been a strenuous day already, and I had a long ways to go. Hot coffee is wonderfully magically restoring and rejuvenating. It's my drug of choice! Sorry, not very sexy, I know. As I sat sipping and studying the guidebook I was joined by two grubby young men hikers who came tumbling down the trail from the summit. I was surprised to see anyone catching me from behind so early in the morning, but obviously they had managed to climb up and over the summit with more speed and agility than I could manage. Well, as Dad always said, old age and deviousness is preferable to youth and beauty any day, and I was there to prove it. They had youth and strength, but I had hot coffee!

Hagerman Overlook, with a view to Mount Mansfield

The boys loved the dogs and the dogs loved them. As we all departed Whiteface Shelter Lyssa and Tina watched mournfully as the young men tumbled on down the trail ahead of us and disappeared into the forest. We were alone again, just the three of us. Slowly but steadily we made good time along the ridge, over Morse Mountain, past Hagerman overlook, through Chilicoot Pass, and then up Madonna Peak.

At Madonna summit the trail traverses developed ski resort country, with mowed ski trails and a lift house at the summit. It was a bit of a relief to rest in the sunshine on the sturdy deck and enjoy the view. I called Hank and checked in. He was happy to hear from me, having not had any communications since I left Johnson yesterday. The bad news was that my phone battery was getting low again. I wasn't sure when I'd be able to get a cell signal again anyhow- there was rough country ahead. He would have to have faith in my abilities and good judgment. Ha, easy enough for me to say, but

not so easy from his end.

After Madonna Summit the trail descends down to Sterling Pond, a popular day hiking area. There is pretty easy access to Sterling Pond from Smugglers Notch, and I began to meet a lot of people on the trail. They were noticeably perky and fresh smelling. They oohed and aahed over the dogs and wanted to know all about where we had come from and how much our packs weighed, and so on. They were amazed to hear that we had walked all the way from Canada! I felt like a pioneer heroine and smelled like one too. Jedediah Smith. Daniel Boone. I couldn't think of any female explorers except maybe Sacajawea, who guided Louis and Clark across the Midwest. I'm a breed apart. I certainly felt like I came from another world compared to the day hikers in their clean colorful spandex and camelbacks.

The trail around Sterling Pond is actually roped off to prevent people from going down to the shoreline and trampling on all of the delicate shoreline vegetation. At a single designated access point you can go down to the water and fill your water bag. There was a slight fishy odor down by the water which I attributed to my lack of having had a hot shower for a week or so. But as I was squeezing a liter of pond water through my filter I glanced down and spotted a dead fish floating by the shore a few feet away. Yuck. I didn't drink the water. It still smelled fishy even after it was filtered.

I hurried away from Sterling Pond, away from the dead fish, the roped off trail boundaries, and away from the (by my wilderness standards) crowds of friendly curious people who made me feel like a side show exhibit ("See the rugged lady through-hiker and her heroic canine companions, hiking all alone in the wilds of the Green Mountains...."). At Elephants Head cliff the trail does a sudden disorienting U-turn and heads due East with no warning. A through-hiker coming up from the other direction assured me that we were still on the trail. It was another very long 2.5 miles down to the highway 108 road crossing. To my surprise we actually caught up with the young men from the Whiteface Shelter, just as they were finishing their lunch break. I schlepped on by them just to have the pleasure of actually passing someone on the trail, but of course my lead didn't last long, and they zipped by me again. The next time I caught them was at the 108 road crossing, which was actually very lucky for them, because the trail had been rerouted and it was not apparent where the trail resumed on the other side of the road. But I had checked out this very spot with my brother in July, and I knew that the southbound trail-head was just around the bend to the left, at the end of a small pullout. I shared this valuable bit of information with the boys, and off they went. "See you at the lodge," they said.

There is a nice parking lot and picnic area at the 108 road crossing. I made good use of the private sit-down privy, and then reorganized my pack a bit, starting off with dumping out the yucky dead fish water from Sterling Pond. I knew there would be plenty to drink on the trail ahead. We were about to embark on the infamous Mt. Mansfield trail. It was only a mile and a half to Taft Lodge, our goal for the night, and it was only 4:30 in the afternoon. Piece of cake. Cake sounded really good.

I had been thinking about Dad a lot. A wise person said that dealing with family is like wrestling with a porcupine in a salt mine. Dad was sentimental as hell and generous to a fault when he wanted to be, but he was impossibly prickly and obstinate the rest of the time. I was particularly vulnerable to his barbs, which is part of the reason I had settled in California, several thousand miles away from him. To my surprise, the instant he passed away I forgave him for every hurt and lash into which he'd ever poured salt, purposely or not. He went back to being the Dad I'd known when I was about five years old- the smartest, strongest, bravest person in the whole world, like Superman. Capable of solving any problem, omniscient, omnipotent and invincible! Now that he had crossed over into the next plane of existence I figured that he would have shed away all of the silly human baggage that made it so difficult for me to get along with him. He'd be able to see right into my soul and know what I was really feeling and how hard I worked and tried to be a good person. I could talk to him and ask him for help and advice without pushing any of his buttons or vice versa.

There were plenty of times when I was taking care of Mom when I wasn't sure of myself, and I'd ask Dad what to do. The answer usually came pretty quickly. We had a deal of sorts. I still had to be strong and work hard, but he'd show me the right path. He pulled strings for me sometimes, and opened doors. Made obstacles go away, or at least seem smaller. On that afternoon as I was getting ready to hike up 1,996 steep rocky vertical feet to the highest summit in Vermont, I was thinking about Dad. By then I had no doubt he was along for the ride. He loved to travel and explore, and while he would never have attempted a 300 mile backpacking trip with a couple of dogs, he was all for adventure. He was seeing the Long Trail through my eyes, I was sure. I was glad for the company- I had an idea that I might need his help on the climb ahead.

I had been keeping an anxious eye on the sky all day. The last forecast I'd seen had been calling for a pretty good chance of rain as the day went on, and I was dreading doing this climb in the rain. I'd had a premonition of struggling up the rocky vertical path with rain pouring down, and the vision had kept me moving and pushing myself all day long. The premonition had seemed so real as to be inevitable, but so far I'd been lucky. Or Dad was somehow holding back the clouds. He could do it of course, he was that strong and clever. The sky was darkening as I crossed 108 and scrambled up the trail. I imagined Dad holding up the clouds like the legendary Dutch boy staving off the flood with his finger in the dike, urging me to hurry up and get going because he couldn't hold it forever.

My top speed when climbing steep & rocky Trail with a full pack is somewhere between 0.5 and 1.0 mph. I calculated that it would take me until 6:30 to reach Taft Lodge, just as we'd be losing daylight. I got the time correct, but missed the mark on the light part. The sky-full of heavily burdened black storm clouds arrived while we were still struggling up the final endless push up to the Taft Lodge. Balancing on the near-vertical line of eroded bedrock comprising the Trail, I tucked away all of my gear into the waterproof inner compartment of my pack. I thought about how lucky I had been with all of the dry weather I'd had so far on my trip, and thought about all of the Vermonters I'd met who were worried because they needed those summer rains. "OK, let 'er rip," I sent the message up to the old man. "Mountains need rain."

The clouds, more burdened than I with their heavy load of moisture, let the bottom drop out. In rapidly dimming light I fought my way up slick wet rock with streamlets of water running down. Quickly drenched from head to toe and wearing only shorts and a tank top, I told myself "I needed a shower, really." It was dangerous to allow myself to get soaking wet, but I knew that the Lodge was only a little bit further up the trail. Lyssa and Tina kept dashing under brush to escape from the pelting rain. "We're almost there, trust me," I assured them over and over, looking into their questioning eyes. I repeated the mantra and kept climbing up when suddenly the dogs both dashed ahead and disappeared up the Trail. When I caught up to them a few minutes later they were in the lodge greeting everyone with their joyous enthusiasm. Other hikers welcomed me. "We knew you were getting close when we saw your dogs," said my young friends from Whiteface. They had arrived just before the downpour and were on the lookout for us. It felt good.

The lodge was dark and full of wet stinky young male hikers. A GMC caretaker offered me fresh strawberries and information by candlelight. She seemed like a goddess to me. I dried off and slipped into warm dry clothes, and fed my faithful companions. They made themselves nests in my pile of gear on the bunk and were gone in no time: sound asleep with full bellies in warm dry soft safe places surrounded by a crowd of earthy-smelly dog-friendly hikers. May their faith in me never be unfounded! It's good to have angels looking out for you, alive or.... otherwise.

When I was a kid I dreamed about being an explorer. I wanted to be a pioneer and ride a horse to Oregon. I wanted to be an Indian living in the wilderness, roaming the forest and the mountains, and sleeping in a tee-pee. I was a little fuzzy about the details of how to implement the whole thing, but when you're 5 years old you don't worry about the details because you have your whole life, which is presumably infinite, to figure it out. Now it was time for me to figure out the details.

I had done quite a bit of day-hiking and short camping trips, a handful of longer backpacking and canoe trips, and one epic 3 week trip down the John Muir Trail the year I turned 50. The dream of through-hiking the Appalachian Trail or Pacific Crest Trail remained a fantasy. In 2015 I read Cheryl Strayed's book "Wild", and thought if she could do it certainly I could too. But Cheryl didn't have a career or a family obligation or a mortgage. She was blessed with a life of hand to mouth poverty and its attendant freedom from material or social debt. Unbounded by a relationship, family, children, career- she was in a sense much freer than I have ever been. Free to spend 8 months walking on a trail.

I misguidedly had equated freedom with having money. For most of my life journey to date, my excuse for never having attempted a through-hike had been financial- I couldn't afford it. I felt I could never afford to take the time off from work, or save up enough money to pay for all of the equipment, food and transportation required for a long trip. What about paying for college tuition, buying a car, paying for housing- all that important basic stuff? How could anyone afford to take all that time off from Life, unless you came from a rich family or had a Trust fund or incredibly supportive family or partner to pay for everything. I was raised to be responsible, pay my bills, get a degree, and aim high on the career ladder. My folks agreed to pay for undergraduate tuition and housing, which was generous enough, as long as I stayed on the straight and narrow. When it came to accepting my responsibilities as an upstanding and productive adult they expected me to be a good citizen of whom they could be proud. Of course I went along with the deal. I liked middle class life with its attendant creature comforts. Going to college and being a good scout seemed like a fair enough exchange for 3 meals a day, a roof overhead and a warm bed, and besides, I liked school. Cornell had hundreds of interesting courses taught by interesting people. I earned a degree and my parents cut me loose. The training wheels came off, and right away it got hard. I had a Bachelor of Arts with a major in American History, a passion for nature and animals, a Volkswagen bug that broke down regularly, no money, no job, and no idea where to go from there.

The first thing I did when I graduated was get a dog. That's the truth. It was spring, senior year, during study week before finals, waiting for graduation day, and my buddy Ellen and I were tooling along the back road across campus in the bug. The radio was playing and Ellen was twiddling the dial when an ad came on for the Thompkins County Animal Shelter listing all of the dogs available for adoption that day. "Hey," said Ellen,"a Gordon Setter mix. Those are cool dogs. We should check it out." Impulse. That's how I got Phoebe. I did a U-turn and headed out the road to the shelter, and that was the beginning of the rest of my life.

That puppy soon became the Most Important Thing in my life. She was all mine and I was all hers, fully responsible for her well-being. She needed dog food, vaccinations, worming, spaying: I got a job. She needed training and house breaking so we began to walk every day, multiple times a day. Phoebe insisted on going outside- a lot. She was a puppy and she loved to run and play, and I was her designated playmate. In the next few months I grew more familiar with Ithaca and its surroundings than I had been for the previous four years of my residence there.

My first job was driving a school bus, which was perfect because I could work a few hours, play with Phoebe, and work for a few more hours, and have the rest of the day to walk with my dog and think. I decided to go back to school in order to take the prerequisite classes I needed in order to apply to vet school. I set my sights on becoming a wildlife veterinarian, but I would only go places where I could take Phoebe. I started dating another bus driver, also a liberal arts graduate with a degree in history, and we got married the next spring. (The wedding was at a park on the lake, and I remember watching Phoebe chasing the geese on the lake shore while a Methodist minister confirmed my commitment to a major misjudgment regarding which I can only say that hindsight is 20:20.) We moved to the west coast, and eventually the state of California admitted me to vet school. Phoebe stood by my side when I divorced my confused and errant bus driver spouse and we chalked the whole thing up to practice. I don't know that I would have survived without the steady and unconditional love and companionship from that sweet dog. I got my DVM and we moved to Long Island to work. And then we moved back again to California. I was looking for something, and I decided it must be a certain gentleman named Hank who was 20 years older than me, who played the guitar and sang sweet sounding music. So we got married again, Phoebe and I.

That was 21 years ago. Now Phoebe was in dog heaven, no doubt hanging out with Mom and Dad who had always adored her. I was still walking an Earthly Trail with Phoebe's successors, my beloved Lyssa and Tina. But there were angels riding on our shoulders. I was never so aware of them as I was that night at Taft Lodge, nor had I ever needed them more.

On the Trail

Chapter 4

September 9, 2016

Day 7
Mount Mansfield

Taft Lodge is the Long Trail's version of a 5-star hotel, complete with a caretaker hostess, and complimentary cookies and strawberries! There is a $5 fee for an overnight stay when the caretaker is in residence- more than a fair deal by my reckoning. I gave her $20 to make up for my wet furry four-footed hiking partners and received a few "end-to-ender" decals as a bonus for my contribution. One decal for each of us. The lodge provided companionship and shelter from the storm, but in my case it was not good for sleeping. I spent most of the night worrying.

I had an endless list of things to worry about. At first I worried about the dogs disturbing other sleepers: what if Lyssa decided to wander around and find a more comfortable spot than the plywood sleeping platform. She loves sleeping bags and often attempted to appropriate them for herself when I hiked with my brothers. Dale's bag was her favorite. But instead of wandering around she had become obsessed with licking the floor for some unknown reason- a steady shlurp, shlurp, shulurp which woke me up and seemed to echo to every corner of the lodge. The only way I could make her stop was to hold on to her collar and restrain her until she gave up and dozed off to sleep. That caused Tina to have to get up and reclaim her fair share of my sleeping pad from which she had been dislodged while I tussled with Lyssa. So when Lyssa's shlurping stopped it was replaced by the resonant sloshing of Tina's heart. Again, I don't know why, but the inflatable mattress acted like a resonating chamber and amplified the sound of anything in contact with it- the rustling of my nylon sleeping bag every time I twitched a muscle, or the grade 5/6 washing machine sound of the heart murmur afflicting my little dog. The sound of a heartbeat is supposed to be soothing and sleep-inducing, but not when your ears are trained to understand the chilling sound of mitral dysplasia. To me it was a reminder of the mortality and vulnerability of my beloved companion. There were lots of other things to worry about that night- the demise of my cell phone which meant that I couldn't call home to reassure my nervous spouse; my lack of a flashlight or headlamp and whether I could make it the 500 yards to the outhouse in the morning given the residual state of flux in my bowels; whether the guy in the bunk overhead would step on us when he got up during the night to go outside and pee. He did climb down about halfway through the night and managed to avoid stepping on us, but when he came back into the lodge he left the door unlatched and it banged repeatedly on its hinges for 45 minutes in the gusting storm winds before someone else stumbled over and latched it. The banging door and gusty wind began to conjure up visions in my imagination of what it would be like to be out hiking the mountain in this weather and be exposed to those fierce erratic gusts. Of immediate concern was the 1/2 mile of trail between Taft Lodge and Mansfield summit. There were several sections of steep exposed cliff with narrow ledges for footholds- would they be slippery in the wetness? A gust of wind would blow us right off the face. I couldn't risk letting the dogs get hurt, and as sure footed as they had proven to be so far, these cliffs were steeper and more exposed than anything we'd faced. It was a long night.

Morning came, and the air was still. The pitch blackness was replaced by dim, misty, dripping swirling fog. I could see just well enough to make it to the outhouse before the other campers woke up and just before my bowels exploded. Phew, one less worry! I fed the dogs, gathered my gear and repacked our packs. We departed with a gang of early risers, shouting thanks and farewell to the caretaker who was still wisely curled up in her cozy bunk, probably dreaming about pancakes. The boys all headed for the "Chin", undeterred by the advice of the guidebook to use the bypass trail in inclement weather. But I was playing it safe for my dogs, and so we turned the other direction, heading for the not-so-exposed bypass- aka "the Profanity Trail."

In the morning it was not raining, probably because Mount Mansfield is inside the clouds. I wondered if it was raining below. The guidebook suggests that hikers might want to go up the Profanity trail in inclement weather, bypassing the steep exposed climb up the Chin. So we cussed our way up the Profanity Trail, through fog and blowing mist. I'm not convinced it was any safer or less strenuous- many times I had to take our packs off and heave them up the ledges, boost the dogs, and then scramble hand over foot myself. But we made it to the top, alive and well and still going strong. I have to say that traversing the summit ridge in blowing mists, with no signs of other human beings in the known world, was way more exciting and adventurous than doing it on a warm, sunny afternoon with 6 or 700 other visitors who arrived via car or gondola."

The profanity trail is a vertical gully, a straight chute to the summit. I guess it's accurate to say that a gully feels less exposed than a steep rounded shoulder of cliffy rock with 2000' feet of open air straight down all around. In a windstorm you would surely have less chance of getting blown off the mountain. But the "bypass" was a really hard climb and we almost didn't make it up a couple of spots, even when I took Lyssa's pack off her. Lyssa doesn't trust me to boost her up without dropping her- she's smart that way. Instead she casts back and forth, searching and studying the rock, and finally making a heroic calculated leap up the face. Sometimes I rush in when she makes her move and help give her a final thrust up. She whined and I cussed. A lot. It was the Profanity trail after all. When we finally made it to the summit most of the other southbound hikers from the lodge had already made it up the Chin route and gone on, and so we had Mansfield ridge to ourselves. That was pretty special, and I found myself once again enjoying the adventure. In July we'd had sunshine, blue skies, spectacular views, and crowds of people. On the morning of September 9th the landscape was surreal and alien- bare, stark, ancient rock formations hidden in swirling, swarming thick wet mists. I felt very alive.

At the "Visitor's Center" near the top parking lot for the toll road, (which is how many of Mansfield's visitors access the summit,) I stopped for my morning coffee and refreshment. I was already feeling tapped out by the early exertions of the day, but the hot coffee revived my spirits. (Have I mentioned that coffee is magical in and of itself, but on the Trail it's even more magical! Synergy, I think!) Once again I studied the map. We had three options. Option one was to continue down the official route of the Long Trail. My brother Dale and I had climbed down this way in July and I knew that there were at least two ladders that descended overhanging boulder faces with no alternate ways around them. The ladders descended into jumbled vertical ravines too steep and too far for Lyssa to jump. No way. Option two was another bypass trail. Again, we had reconnoitered this route in July, circling back up the bypass on our return to descend the mountain to the car. That afternoon in July we had been caught in a torrential rainstorm while on the bypass, which had turned the trail into a flash flood of slippery rock. Incredibly slippery. There is a lot of exposed rock on the Long Trail, (have I mentioned there is a lot of exposed rock?!), but for the most part it is not slippery, even when it is wet, because it is well traveled enough so that the thin layer of algae is constantly worn away, resulting in a clean surface that affords enough friction to allow firm purchase to the sole of your shoe. But the less traveled bypass trails are slimy with algae, and when it is wet they are as slippery as ice, and treacherous. A caretaker had warned me- in all of her years hiking in the Green Mountains the only place she'd ever been injured was the south Mansfield Bypass Trail- she'd sprained an ankle and had to be carried down the mountain. I might not have believed her except that Dale and I had been there and done that, without the sprained ankle but close enough. The bypass trail would be slick and dangerous. The aforementioned caretaker had recommended a third alternative, which was to take the Maple Ridge Trail to the Whompahoofous Trail and circle around back to the Long Trail via Butler Lodge. She said there were a couple of rough spots, but of the three alternatives she thought that would be the best way to go with the dogs. So the Whompahoofous it was.

We made it down, getting pretty Whomped in the process. There were no impossible ladders, although there was plenty of steep exposed bedrock shoulder type territory. The crux was a gigantic slab of rock that had broken loose from impossibly ancient billion year old bedrock bones of the mountain. You couldn't go around it or over it. You had to go through it. Under the slab and through the crevice. We barely squeaked through it. I took Lyssa's pack off of her so that she wouldn't get lodged in the crevice and somehow she picked a way through the mess of boulders, cracks and crevices. She's my hero dog. So is Tina. When we got to Butler Lodge Lyssa stole a piece of bread and butter from the resident caretaker- right off her plate. I let her, apologizing insincerely. I was busy borrowing a cell phone from a passing day hiker so that I could send a message to Hank that we were safe and well and had successfully crossed Mount Mansfield. Life was good.

I make a habit of asking everyone I meet about ladders. Lyssa can leap up 4 foot faces and scramble up steep rocky ravines, but she can't do vertical ladders, and I can't carry her up or down them. So far we haven't encountered anything that she can't scramble up or down or around, but we bypassed the worst of the steep ladders on Mansfield, and there are rumors of more ladders ahead. Camel's Hump, Ladder Gap, Stark Mountain.....But today, Mansfield, the highest peak in Vermont, is behind us! We celebrate with a large bag of Tuna, split 3 ways! And some chocolate covered blueberries for me. Southbound, we roll!

The storm clouds give way to sunshine and blue skies as we descend. At some point during the day I become aware of great booming noises. They get louder and louder, occurring in repetitive bursts. Maybe the Forest Service is blowing something up. It sounds like cannon fire. It is cannon fire. I find the answer on my map- Ethan Allen Firing Range. Ugh, how awful and intrusive. The repetitive booming disturbs the quiet peace and serenity to which I have become accustomed. I remind myself that part of Vermont history includes Minute Men, Green Mountain Boys and Loyalists, all of whom would have no doubt been members of the NRA. The day is salvaged by the fact that the booming stopped before sunset and I arrive at Puffer Shelter in time to enjoy the glorious view of the valley below, and watch the colors of the alpenglow fade through the whole spectrum of orange, red, pink, purple, lavender and gray. Perhaps the peace and quiet of the evening is accentuated by the fact that the cannon fire has stopped. I don't know; I'm still glad to be there. Maybe someday we won't need guns at all, and the booming will stop for good. Maybe. Trail Magic happens.

I really liked Puffer Shelter. It is situated on the northeast face of Bolton Mountain at about 3000' elevation in such a way that it offers an excellent view over the rolling

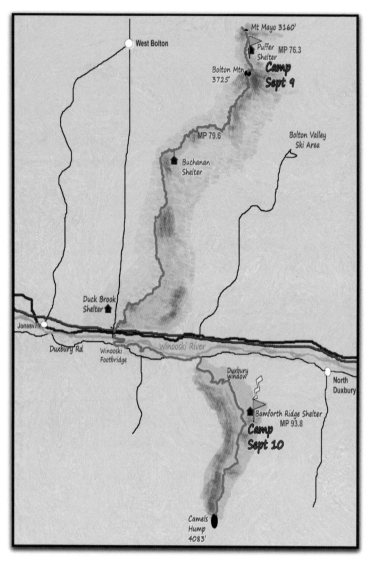

**Map 5: Bolton Mtn, the Winooski River, and
Bamforth Ridge**

green country below, a rare treat on those thickly forested summits. But the previous night had instilled me with an aversion to sleeping on a wooden platform, no matter how enticing the view, and so I pitched our tent on a level spot a few hundred feet above the lean-to. I used the shelter as a kitchen and dining room, and as I sat sipping soup and admiring the kaleidoscopic color show of alpenglow in the eastern sky I was joined by two young men backpackers who came tumbling down the trail from Bolton summit. They were as cheerful and friendly as they could be, but after a bit I left them to the lean-to and the girls and I retreated to our little tent up the hill.

Fortunately I had forgotten that Puffer Shelter was a dry camp, or I would have unnecessarily exhausted myself carrying a lot of extra water up the hill. The regular creek that supplied water to campers had dried up with the end of summer, but the storm that drenched us on Mansfield had also left puddles and pools of fresh water in the creek-bed, and Lyssa had no trouble finding them and showing me where they were. With Mansfield behind us and feeling well fed and hydrated, I was able to relax and take time to enjoy the evening. Alone, but not lonely, I simply sat and appreciated the colors of the land and sky. It was so beautiful- a gradient of green, blue green, gray green, purple green, lavender, rose, pink and orange, all fading to gray and then black, as the earth became indistinguishable from the sky. Such a beautiful planet. It was heavenly. Heaven on Earth. This planet is heaven, I think. When you die and go to heaven, maybe this is where you come. That would be fine with me. Sitting lightly on my shoulders, I heard my angels agree.

Before nodding off for the night I glanced at the map. After a quick steep early climb to the summit of Bolton we had 10 miles of downhill, all the way down to the Winooski River Valley, at 326' elevation, the lowest point on the Long Trail. The Trail crossed the river and then meandered along to the east for nearly 3 miles before entering Camel's Hump State Park and heading south again. Camping was not permitted along the river or within the first mile or so of the State Park. But if everything went well and we made good time on the long downhill, I thought we might make it pretty far into the park, maybe even to Bamforth Ridge Shelter at the 17 mile mark. I didn't want to worry about finding a place to camp tomorrow. It would work out. I was going to enjoy those 10 miles of downhill. Tonight we would sleep.

Sept 10, 2016

Day 8
Bolton to Bamforth

I don't remember the first half mile of Day 7, but according to the map it was 1/2 mile of straight up scrambling. All I know is that I was eager to get to the summit because I knew that the next 10 miles would be all downhill, which was wonderful because I felt driven to catch up on some mileage. I wanted to get across the Winooski River. If I failed to make it to the river I'd have to stop well before my 10 mile minimum in order to find a decent safe camping spot and be well away from the highway, and I needed to start doing a lot better than that if I was going to be able to finish the Trail on time. But once we got across the Winooski it was a good 5 miles to the next shelter and "legal" campsite at Bamforth Ridge. We needed to aim for at least 15 miles today, or more if we were to make it to Bamforth Ridge. Having 10 miles of downhill on the day's agenda gave us a shot at making it to Bamforth Ridge.

The long descent from Bolton summit was indeed a treat after the Mansfield experience. First came the usual slippery scramble down the eroded vertical cliffs and boulders, watching every step and foothold, carefully placing my trekking pole, balancing, pivoting, grasping hand-holds polished by a thousand hands before me, and occasionally taking off my pack and sliding down on my butt. To my astonishment the descent now seemed fairly routine and predictable, with none of the grueling exposed ledges and shoulders or narrow crevices we'd encountered on Mansfield. The steepness abated as we reached the transition zone where thick spruces began to give way to broadleaved birches and maples. We didn't stop; we were going downhill, making good time. The anxiety I always feel at the higher elevations receded and my confidence returned in the dry, lambent air of the lower elevation forest.

But 10 miles is a long ways for me, even when it's mostly downhill. The last 5 or so miles before the bridge over the Winooski River were dry and endless, and stopping to camp was not an option due to lack of water sources. By the time we finally emerged onto Bolton Notch Road later in the afternoon I was tired and hot. Tina and Lyssa trotted along steadily as if they could go forever; I was the only pack member feeling the strain of the non-stop push.

Finally we crossed under Interstate 89 through a tunnel. I loved the tunnel. There was something oddly Felliniesque about the juxtaposition of an ultralight foot traveler, accompanied by 2 free-wheeling four-footed fur-balls, striding along 20 feet below, while tons and tons of com-busting-fossil-fuel-propelled machinery hurtled along over the earth overhead at 90 miles an hour. I imagined jaded drivers slouched at the wheel, bored passengers focused on their tablets and phones, idly poking at their screens- I didn't envy them in the least! They were in a totally different world than I, remote, isolated in their machine bubbles, their thoughts in cyberspace. I was grounded, alive, and intimately connected to the earth. Although I was a product of that 90 mile an hour machine world above, I had achieved a degree of separation from it. Eventually I would return to it, but for now I was an earth crawler, more kin to the wild animals and forest dwellers than to the humans whizzing along the narrow asphalt trail overhead. And I was free to go where I pleased, under my own power. The only thing separating me from my planet was a thin layer of cushiony rubber. I was still burdened by my need for the gear that I carried on my back, but that was nothing compared to the burdens of a car, a home, a mortgage, and a career. I was truly in a different world than I'd been in a few weeks ago, which made me start thinking about the idea that there really are different planes of existence, according to our perceptions of reality, and maybe more planes above and beyond life as we know it. For the past few years my husband Hank has been on a spiritual quest to get in touch with other planes of existence. His vehicle is not a man-made machine, but through the practice of meditation. I cynically referred to it as staring at the inside of your eyelids for the meaning of life. Irreverent, I knew, but I'm happy with seeing what is in this Earthly world and experiencing it to the fullest extent I possibly can. God isn't pasted on the inside of your eyelids, I told him. God is out there in the forests and in the Mountains.

Spiritual planes. And that made me start thinking about Mom and Dad being on their new adventure somewhere in the next world, beyond the veil as they say, and I realized that I wasn't thinking about them as much as I had been. Or at least, I wasn't obsessing about their last few months of life as I had been before I set out for the east coast. Instead my mind was occupied with the Trail, and the forest, and watching my steps, keeping an eye on Lyssa and Tina, the weather, the next water source, and always watching the miles. Adding up the distance I had come and the distance I had left to go and how many hours were left in the day. At the bridge I studied the map again. The trail has been rerouted here, and I needed to be careful not to loose it. I figured I had enough time to make it to Bamforth Ridge, but not if I wasted time getting lost and searching around for the trail blazes. Pushing away the impulse dwell in the past and revisit my parents' last few years of life, I focused on the Trail instead. The heavenly plane would have to wait awhile yet.

The Trail has indeed been rerouted between the suspension bridge and the next southbound trail-head on the other side of Duxbury Road, which is 2 miles down the road to the east. Instead of routing the trail along the road, which is unpleasant and dangerous walking, the Long Trail dives down into private land between culti-vated fields and the riparian zone along the riverbank. I appreciate the efforts that went into this arrangement- no doubt the result reflects loads of research, communi-cations and negotiations by the good folks at the Green Mountain Club. I was very grateful that the dogs and I didn't have to walk on the shoulder of the road, dodging cars and breathing exhaust. Instead we tromped along the edge of giant fields with cabbage and mown hay on the right side, and willows and brambles on the left. The air was humid and reeking of mud and willows. We were amongst the groundhogs, deer and field mice, living on the fringes, in the transition zones. Ready to bolt into the safety of the brush. We crossed several fences using clev-erly designed stepladders. These giant sawhorse shaped constructs are no problem for humans and agile little ter-riers, but Lyssa had a little trouble with the up and down ladder concept at first. We took our time and she stayed focused with me, watching, trying it out, testing the foot-holds, and making it over safely. By the last sawhorse she confidently led the way up and over as if she had been doing it all her life. Agility shepherd. I was delighted with her achievement. At home there is a dog agility training club, with a man-made obstacle course. It's fun, but this was the real deal, and my dogs were Aces!

Eventually the Trail rejoins the road for another half mile or so before finally reaching the large parking lot for the trail head into Camel's Hump State Park. White blazes were few and far between and I was in constant mount-ing anxiety that we had missed a turn and would up in Duxbury, far from where we wanted to be. But suddenly we reached the gap and the parking lot. Hallelujah! Only 5.2 miles to go to Bamforth Ridge shelter. We can do this. I thought.

The Winooski River valley is at 362 feet in elevation, the

lowest point on the Long Trail. There was nowhere to go except up, the afternoon was wearing on and was tired. I studied the map and picked out my mileage markers. A bridge, the cascade, the Duxbury window. Halfway there. Dragging myself uphill, I was pushing as fast as I could to make it before dark. The trail got steeper and steeper, and the last mile felt endless. It seemed that I would never get there before the light faded away. I felt like it was Mt. Mansfield all over again, but without the pouring rain. It was nearly dark when I stumbled into the intersection for the side trail to the shelter. The water hole was a steep climb down to a water pipe with a trickle of water coming out. Even though my body insisted it was finished, there was more work to do. I had no choice but to climb down to the spring with all of my water bags and containers and lug them back up to my tent so that I could make dinner and give the dogs water overnight, and still have some for myself in the morning. I set up my tent on a designated tent platform in gray gloomy dusk. Luckily it was all a regular routine: measure out the dog food, make sure Tina gets her heart pill, blow up the sleeping pad and spread out the bag (which was immediately claimed by Tina,) heat the water for my dinner of potato soup and a handful of dried fruit and nuts, mix up a liter of instant milk- half for now and half in the morning with protein powder, keep one liter of water aside in its special spot in the corner of the tent for drinking during the night, finally brush my teeth and I'm almost done. One last pit stop and look around to make sure all of the dog stuff and gear is stowed safely away in it's usual assigned place, and I can lay my tired self down. Finally. Rest. It was a good day. A long hard day of constant pushing to meet my goal; I barely made it, but I made it. Rest. Tomorrow is the Hump, tonight I can rest. I gave a brief nod to my guardian angels for getting me to Bamforth Ridge Shelter, and then nod off to sleep, curled up between my gear and Lyssa and Tina.

Most of the day was downhill; I logged 17.5 miles, my longest day yet. Maybe there's hope for this old lady. I pulled into Bamforth Ridge shelter with about 45 minutes of daylight left to spare- barely enough to fetch water and set up my tent. I tented because when I came around the corner and peeked into the shelter I was greeted by a row of frowzy, dreamy-eyed young men. They were friendly and harmless enough, but I knew I would not sleep well with so much company. Besides, I toss and turn a lot and usually have to get up a few times during the night, and I don't want to have to worry about disturbing other people. I had never set up my tent on a platform before, but it turned out to be pretty easy; the platform was nice and level and just the right size. It was also quiet and well removed from the shelter. I re-read the notes about the trail over Camel's Hump, look ahead to where I might expect to camp the following night, set my alarm for 5:30 and drift off....

Chapter 5

Sept 11, 2016

Day 9
Storm

A little before 5:00 I woke up to flashing lights and crashing booms. For a moment I thought I had stumbled into the firing range again. Then I realized that a thunderstorm was fast approaching, and decided would be prudent to make a mad dash out to pee before it hit. Lyssa and Tina had the same idea, and together we ran out to do our business in the bush. Tina and I dove back into the tent just as the rain started, but Lyssa did not. I stuck my head out of the tent to call her but by then the storm was on us and my voice was drowned out by the rain and crashing thunder. I tried counting the number of seconds between lightening strikes and thunder rolls, but there was no gap at all. The cell was directly overhead!

People who engage in high risk sports- mountain climbing, base jumping, sky diving, tight-rope walking- often confess to being addicts. They are addicted to endorphins. Endorphins are natural chemicals which are produced by the body itself. You don't have to inject them or swallow a pill. You just have to trick your glands into releasing them into your bloodstream. This happens under conditions when the body perceives itself to be at high risk for injury or death. Endorphins are released and suddenly you feel better- braver, stronger, calmer- and not bothered by pain.

Endorphin addicts claim that they only feel "alive" by risking death. The trick is to come as close as you can to the edge without tipping over to the other side: waiting until the last second to pull the rip-cord on the parachute, or plunging off a cliff with a bungee cord attached to your ankle calculated to stop your fall a half an inch from the ground. After all, it's not the fall that kills you, it's the landing. Thrill-seekers.

I am not a thrill-seeker. I feel plenty alive enough just being here walking around on this little planet. I generally enjoy a good thunderstorm, however. I used to love watching summer afternoon storms blow in across Lake Ontario when we were kids spending our summers at camp. We'd sit out on the old davenport on the back porch and watch the sky darkening, counting the seconds between the flashes of lightening and the crashes of thunder. Each second counted meant it was how many miles away? How fast was it approaching? Sudden gusts of wind sprang up just as the rain hit, and the little kids would run inside for fear of getting drenched by the ferocious rain driving in sideways through the screens. Braver kids stayed outside, watching until the lightening was striking right overhead in deafening claps of thunder. We huddled together in the safety of the davenport cushions, until suddenly there was a slight, perceptible lessening in the force of the wind. The split second gap between thunder and lightening began to lengthen as the cell retreated, as if the great booming rumbling monster was dragging its heels behind its flashy partner. Spears of light forging the path while slower, clumsy, tag-along Thunder trundled along in its wake. Nothing left to do at that point but for the rest of the kids to follow the others into the cabin, have some popcorn or fresh-baked cookies, and join in the perpetual game of Monopoly or curl up with a cheap paperback. If Dad was around we might be subject to a physics lesson: why does light travel at a different speed than sound, why does the gap between light-ening and thunder get closer as the storm approaches, why does the whistle on a train change in pitch when the train is moving? How do you know if it's getting closer or further away? Understanding physics made the storm a little less scary, but no less thrilling to behold. Sitting on the back porch of the cabin watching a summer storm roll across Lake Ontario was plenty thrilling for me. I needed no more endorphins to feel very much alive.

But now here I was sitting on an 8'x8' platform on a ridge in a forest in Vermont, with a flimsy sleeping bag and pad instead of a cozy cushioned davenport, and nothing but a piece of hyperlight fabric over my head to protect me and my small collection of gear that was crucial in keeping me alive and mobile for the next 200 miles.

Torrential rain. This was the first time my tent had been in the rain, and while I had read plenty of on-line reviews about how watertight it was, I wasn't sure quite what to expect. I gathered my gear around me, hunkered down and hugged Tina, who is gun-shy and was shaking like she'd swallowed a popcorn maker with a short-circuit. I was worried that my gear was going to get soaked. I was worried that Tina's heart would pound so hard that it would explode. I was worried that the storm would turn into an all day downpour, and my quest to finish the Trail by the 23rd would be dashed. I would have worried about being struck by lightening if it had occurred to me, but it didn't. Fortunately. I worried about all of those things so that I would not worry about the thing that worried me the most- where the hell was Lyssa?

Suddenly my mind began replaying the pre-flight safety lecture the flight attendants give when an airplane is preparing to take off. I'd heard it a hundred times: "place your oxygen mask firmly over your mouth and nose be-fore helping others around you." Right. I had to take care of me before I could take care of anything else. I couldn't afford to worry about Lyssa right then. The biggest danger was that I would get wet if the tent leaked or blew down. If I got wet, I would get cold, and if my gear got wet I would have no way to warm up. Hypothermia kills. That was probably my biggest risk. Of course, a tree could also fall down and crush my tent, but there was nothing I could do about that. With conscious effort I relinquished control over that possibility to a higher power, along with the slim chance that the tent would get struck by lightening. I gave it up to Dad. He always kept us safe! Thinking of Dad reminded me of those afternoon physics lessons and I started purposely watching the lightening flashes and counting seconds until I heard crashes of thunder.

Simply stepping back and observing the storm changed my perspective from helpless victim to detached observer. Rational thought resumed. Keep dry, protect my gear. Water was creeping in under the tent flap, creeping along the ground cloth; a small puddle was sneaking up along towards my sleeping bag. I stuffed the bag into its sack and crammed it into my waterproof pack, quickly followed by my down pants and sweater, maps, cell phone and extra socks. Thoughtfully I pulled on a few layers of clothing and then my waterproof pants and jacket over top. Felt a little silly sitting inside the tent like that. All dressed up and going nowhere. But I was ready. Oxygen mask in place; ready to help others.

Sitting cross-legged on the pad with Tina in my lap and the rain pelting down on the tent I remembered a day years ago when I had only had Lyssa for a week or so. I had adopted her from my county animal shelter, where I worked. She was about a year old, and had been picked up at the local WalMart parking lot, which is a popular spot for dumping unwanted animals in our county. She was perfect: friendly, well-mannered, and had a sweet, mellow disposition. We could not believe that she had been dumped, but nobody called or came looking for this beautiful animal. During her holding period in the shelter I visited with her often and every time I left I could feel her eyes following me. "Take me with you," her eyes pleaded. The day before I took her home I had a vision of she and I on a trail together. It was a vision so clear and sharp- all I had to do was follow my intuition and it would become manifest. A week later we were on a conditioning hike around a lake near my home on the west slope of the Sierra Nevada Mountains. Lyssa, (named after an elegant telepathic dragon in a novel I read), loved it. I cautiously let her off leash so that she could stretch out a bit. It was a joy to watch her move. She stayed close by and always came running when I called her. Perfect! I was about 7 miles around the 9 mile perimeter of the lake when my cell phone rang- a surprise call from my sister in New Jersey! Distracted, I missed a trail marker and wandered up on a side trail. 20 minutes later I finished my call, realized my mistake, and started working my way back to the lake trail. Lyssa was no longer with me. I backtracked, calling and whistling- no dog. I hiked up several side trails, bellowing and whistling. I met hikers coming the other direction and asked them if they had seen her- no one had. To make matters worse a cold front was moving in, bringing rain and dropping temperatures. The rain turned to snow. Big wet heavy flakes. Still no dog. I decided to finish the trip around the lake and return to my car and put up some signs with my phone number. Surely someone would find her and see my signs, or call the animal shelter. I would get her back. I reached the car and was scrabbling around for a pen and paper when I looked up to see the most wonderful and unbelievable sight- my dog trotting confidently up the middle of the road towards the car. I opened the door and she hopped in, licked my nose, and shook wet snow all over the interior of the car. I grabbed her in a bear hug! She was mine and I was hers. She had gone ahead of me on the main trail but when I didn't show up behind her she backtracked to try to find me, missing the side trail and going all 7 miles back around the lake the way we had come, ending up at the car. That was 4 years and many miles ago. Since then we have kept a better eye on each other! Surely she was not lost in this wild forest, so far from home, terrified by this tremendous storm, running in blind panic down Bamforth Ridge, no, no, no. My trip was over. I would spend the rest of my life searching the Green Mountains for my shepherd. I would put posters at every trail-head and ads in every newspaper in Vermont. The trip was a disaster.

The Hump

I notice lights again but this time it is not more lightening bolts from the storm. Drops still beat an irregular rhythm on the tent, but it's water dripping off the trees, not rain. The rain has stopped and the brightness is..... dawn! Tina is sound asleep in my lap. I unzip the tent flap and call Lyssa. After a few seconds she hops in and to my amazement her coat is dry! Incredible wonderful brilliant unbelievable Dog! She licks me all over and I want to hug her forever. I am so lucky. My dog is not lost, and the worst thing that could happen did not happen. It's a great day for a hike!

Endorphins. I had 'em. After the storm passed I admit I felt pretty great. Ready to hike, ready for Camel's Hump. Not only had I survived a thunderstorm passing about 30 feet over my head, I was dry, alive and mobile! My dogs were safe, fed and with me on the trail- "Southbound, We Roll," I shouted!

That was how the day started. I played it safe, and took the Alpine Trail, bypassing the Hump altogether. I will go back and do the summit some other time, without the dogs, on a clear sunny day when I can enjoy the legendary view. The ladders and steep exposed cliffs sound like fun too, but I've pushed the envelope enough already today. By the time I reach the descent down the Monroe Trail the sun is shining and the mountain is crawling with day-hikers. Morning must have been a crazy dream. At Montclair Glen I catch up with 3 of the young men who were at the Bamforth Ridge Shelter last night. They are relaxed and congenial. One of

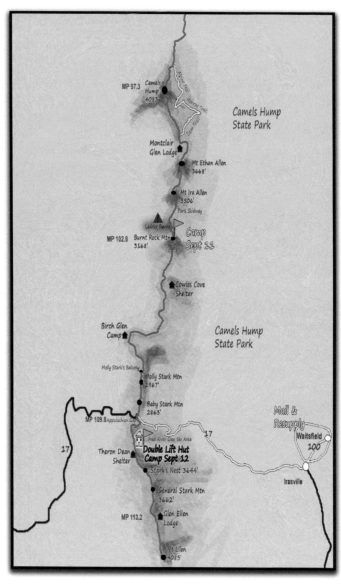

MP 97.3 Camels Hump 4083'

Alpine Trail

Monroe Trail

Dean Trail

Camels Hump State Park

Montclair Glen Lodge

Mt Ethan Allen 3668'

Mt Ira Allen 3506'

Paris Skidway

Ladder Ravine

MP 102.8 Burnt Rock Mtn 3168'

Camp Sept 11

Cowles Cove Shelter

Birch Glen Camp

Camels Hump State Park

Molly Stark's Balcony

Molly Stark Mtn 2967'

Baby Stark Mtn 2863'

MP 109.8 Appalachian Gap

Mad River Glen Ski Area

17

Mail & Resupply

Waitsfield 100

17

Theron Dean Shelter

Double Lift Hut Camp Sept 12

Stark's Nest 3644'

General Stark Mtn 3662'

Irasville

Glen Ellen Lodge

MP 113.2

Mt Ellen 4083'

Map 6: Camels Hump, Ladder Ravine, Burnt Rock Mtn, The Starks, Waitsfield, and Mad River Glen Ski Area

them says what a smart dog my shepherd is, who spent the thunderstorm hanging out with them in the shelter. She disappeared as soon as it stopped raining, he says. "Smart" doesn't even come close to what my dog is, but I can't find the right words either. Trail Magic. Lyssa!

Leaving Bamforth Ridge Shelter we found the world had been transformed into a different place than the world we traveled through yesterday. Perhaps it was the storm- it was easy to imagine the power of that lightening and thunder striking so closely overhead had somehow boosted us into another plane of existence! Certainly I felt energized and almost ecstatic to be alive and hiking up the ridge towards Camel's Hump Peak. We climbed up through the forest, periodically emerging onto open shoulders of exposed bedrock. Everything was gray- gray rock and gray mist swirling all around. We walked and climbed, eyes peeled for those beautiful white blazes marking the trail through the greyness. Sometimes the clouds would coalesce into brief showers. Occasionally thunder rumbled in the distance. I stayed dry in my rain-gear. After an hour or so I stopped and heated up some water for a hot cup of coffee. It tasted divine, and not long after that we arrived at the turn-off for the Alpine Trail, which served as a foul weather bypass route. I planned to take that route regardless of the weather in order to avoid the exposed ladder descents down the cliffs on the south face of the Hump, but it was some consolation to think that I wouldn't be missing the view from the summit due to the thick cloud bank settled over the mountain.

The Alpine trail was narrow and brushy- obviously not well traveled. But the worst part was the boulders were coated with algae and as slick as ice. I went down hard a couple of times, unexpectedly, cussing. It was a long 1.2 miles, and at one point we emerged onto an exposed shoulder with a view of the summit about a half mile due west of us. The clouds were beginning to break up and I caught a few shadowy glimpses of human figures whooping and waving on the summit. The boys from the lean-to. I was a little envious of their summit, but I had my girls with me, which was more than a fair trade.

Presently we reached the Monroe Trail, and the scene shifted again. In an instant it seemed the sky was blue, the day was warm and sunny, and there were groups of people everywhere! It was the weekend, and swarms of day hikers were out taking advantage of one of the last sunny days of the summer to climb Camel's Hump. Feeling a bit like an unworldly alien creature caught in the city freeway during rush hour, Lyssa and Tina and I joined the masses on the Monroe Trail. After 9 days on the trail we were grubby and stinky compared to the colorful clusters of fragrant day hikers, bouncing and chattering their way down the trail. Alternate realities. I was relieved to reach the turn for the Dean Trail, and be alone again. The Dean Trail was not named for Howard Dean, the Democrat who briefly ran for president in 2004, but I thought about him anyhow while I was on it. He is the only politician to whom I have ever donated money. He was instrumental in securing legislative support for the Trail years before he ran for president, so it's okay. Before we rejoined the Long Trail we stopped in a meadow for a rest and a snack, and then Camel's Hump was behind us.

Now that a second formidable 4000' peak is behind me I should be feeling relief that the worst is over. But there is one more challenge ahead, and it is getting closer with every step we take. Back at Taft Lodge, eating strawberries with the GMC caretaker, she had helped me work out my strategies for getting safely over Mt. Mansfield and Camel's Hump. Then as an afterthought she added- "there is one spot that could be trouble for you- a little further on past Camel's Hump there is a place called Ladder Gap. There's an aluminum house painting ladder that goes straight up an overhang. Most people traveling with dogs have to carry their dogs down it. But you might have trouble with Lyssa."

Several of the north bound hikers at the table are nodding and murmuring in agreement. "I don't want to scare you," she says, scaring me, "but it would suck if you got down in there and got stuck. Of course, you made it this far so you'll probably be fine," she adds, reassuringly. There must be a way around it, right? I say. After all, hikers have been hiking this trail for a long time before they brought up aluminum ladders. Everyone agrees that there must be a way around the ladder, but nobody actually saw anything obvious.

So for the past few days while I was focused on getting over Mansfield and the Hump (or Rump, as I now call it), the thought of Ladder Gap was lurking in the background. Now it fills my brain completely and I know I won't be able to think of anything else until I deal with it. One of the north-bounders I met had 2 dogs, and I quizzed him about the ladder. He simply hoisted up the border collie, tucked it under his arm like a football, and carried him down. He had a hiking companion, who had helped with the old Labrador. They are big strong guys, twice my size. They look at Lyssa and shrug. They are honest; they don't have an easy answer. They wish me luck but it's not their problem. It's my hike and my problem. I took a chance, choosing for my hiking partner this giant dog who I cannot carry. Plenty of people bring dogs on the Long Trail according to everything I had read, but nothing had specifically addressed the unique issues that might confront 58 year old ladies hiking alone with 85 pound shepherds.

On to Ladder Gap. First climb Mount Ethan Allen, then Ira Allen, and we are getting closer. Paris Skidway. Onward. The Trail is rough, but not too bad. Soon we will be climbing Burnt Rock Mountain. We drop into a ravine and the Trail takes a 90 degree turn to the right. 100' ahead in a dim green rocky chasm there is the Ladder, going straight up. I feel like Jack, gazing up the beanstalk. The ladder doesn't exactly disappear into the clouds, but it might as well. It's tall, and the cliff is overhanging. Everything in the ravine is green and covered with moss except for the Ladder, which is shiny silver. It's an impressive sight. "Shit," I say.

My plan is to drop the packs at the bottom of the ladder, find an alternate way up the cliff with the dogs, and then go back to the top of the ladder, tie up the dogs, and climb back down to retrieve the packs. But first I can't resist a quick climb up the ladder just for fun. I trot up the rungs and Tina beats me to the top! Remember I said she was a 5.4 free-climber? Make that 5.9. I couldn't do what she just did- leap straight up 3 feet to a tiny ledge, skitter along the side of the ladder, bounce once or twice and wiggle the last couple feet to the top of the ledge. I tell her she isn't supposed to go up until we figure out how to get Lyssa up, and she beats me back down to the bottom. No problem. Meanwhile Lyssa is pacing back and forth at the foot of the ladder, whining anxiously. She knows this is trouble.

I tell Lyssa the plan- "we go back and forth along the bottom of the cliff until we find a way up, okay? We can do this." Sounds good to her. This time the Trail is not taunting me. This is just a little ravine, and the ladder is not her doing. She's on my side now. We can do this. We explore up and down the ravine, looking for a route that Lyssa can handle. On the fourth trip up the ravine we keep going until I see that the cliff looks less formidable, and there is a spot where maybe we can traverse a few boulders, and if we're lucky and don't fall into a crevasse then we can try to scramble up a steep rocky gully. Everything is covered with thick moss, and the "gully" is full of brush, dead branches, and logs scattered like pick up sticks. I can't be sure if my footings will hold or crumble away in avalanches of dirt and moss. Lyssa is ahead of me, picking her own way. Sure of herself now, she pulls ahead and shoots up to the top. I am right behind her, with Tina encouraging me. Up we go. Then down through thick spruce, farther than I expected, until we are back on the Trail again, the beautiful Trail. I

102

retrieve our packs, and soon we are happily climbing Burnt Rock Mountain. Not a care in the world!

It's late and I am looking for a level place to pitch the tent, but I also need to find water. In my obsession to get past the Ladder, I had neglected to think about preparing for the night's camp. But there is not a rivulet or so much as a square foot of level ground anywhere on the climb up Burnt Rock Mountain, so we can't stop. The summit is exposed bedrock, revealing a gorgeous view and the Presidential Range glowing purple against the skyline. I wish I could stop and enjoy the beauty of this place. Although I am in a hurry to find a good camp spot before dark, I pause for a moment. I deserve a few minutes to savor this view. It's been a long, eventful day, with two big challenges and a pre-dawn monster thunderstorm to top it off. As I admire the view I realize that I am standing on the only level ground within miles, and Lyssa and Tina are drinking their fill from a basin of fresh rainwater caught by the bedrock during this morning's storm. There are puddles everywhere and I have found my home for the night. What a perfect way to end this most adventurous day, with the whole of Eastern Vermont rolled out below me.

Sept 12, 2016

Day 10
Waitsfield

Summits. Who doesn't love them? People put themselves in mortal danger and sometimes even die trying to reach a mountain top. I like the view from a summit because it helps me to keep things in perspective. All of my worries and obsessions get small and insignificant when I look at them from the top of a mountain. Of course there's also a nice sense of accomplishment and satisfying physical exhaustion following a day of hiking in the high peaks. Together they make the Zen of a Summit. But summits aren't great places for getting a good night's sleep. They are cold- a lot colder than the trail going up or down. And frequently they are windy. Currents of air get pinched and squeezed by the rising land. By the time it reaches the ridge line a large volume of air might get compressed in a narrow plane, forcing it to move at a high velocity in order to spill over into the space on other side. The wind tears over the summit, howling and whistling through the trees and crags.

As the sun disappeared behind us, on the summit of Burnt Rock Mountain the temperature began to drop. I gobbled down my hot potato soup and between bites I layered up with every article of clothing I had with me. I was particularly thankful for the down pants! Lyssa excavated herself a sheltered den under the stunted vegetation and Tina curled up inside my sleeping bag. She only does that when it's really cold. She's a dog thermometer. The colder the night, the deeper she goes. I hurried through the evening routine of arranging all the gear in it's usual places, filled the water bottles, and slithered into the bag with Tina. I didn't bother to set up the tent because it would have meant a lot of work rearranging rocks and finding vegetation to which to secure it on the bare rock summit, and I didn't think it would be good for the sensitive alpine ecosystem. Instead I found a semi-protected level spot between two outcrops, just big enough for the sleeping pad. Even though my spot was protected from the wind, I might have been warm with the added protection of the tent shell.

It was a rough night. Fully enclosed in the bag with a tiny air hole for my nose, I was barely warm enough. Tina helped, but it was definitely a more than one-dog night. Gusts of wind howled and whistled like a flock of banshees flying over the crest. No sooner did I manage to doze off, when another bout of howling and whistling would ensue. The worst part was that every time I woke up I would have the irresistible urge to roll over. This meant disturbing Tina from wherever she had wedged herself, and flipping her over to the other side so that I could curl around her again. Then I'd have to find my nose hole again, all the while trying not to slide off the mattress pad. If I was lucky I might doze off for awhile, maybe 5 minutes, or an hour if I was really lucky. Around midnight the wind started to abate. The stillness was blessed. The wind was still putting up a fight but eventually the periods of stillness grew longer, and I could hear Tina's heartbeat - resonant and sloshing- echoing through the air mattress. So fragile and precious, a silky and warm ball tight against me.

Morning came. The sky began to lighten. Lyssa was nosing at the opening to my sleeping bag, looking for my face to lick. Ready to start the day. I fumbled around with the drawstring on the mummy bag and got it open so that Tina could dash out to do her business. I looked to the east to see the color of the sunrise but I was having some trouble seeing the horizon-something was wrong- my eyelids were swollen shut and I couldn't open them. I pried them open with cold fingers. The sky was glowing purple. Beautiful! I massaged my eyelids and crawled out of the bag to move around and do some stretches- I needed to get my circulation moving to relieve the edema in my eyelids. The only way I could see was to hold my eyes open with my thumb and forefinger. My throat was dry and scratchy and my lymph nodes felt swollen and tender. Later my eye doctor told me she thought that my eyelids had adhered to my corneas because of exposure and dehydration, but I don't know. I wanted to get packing and start heading down the mountain, but obviously I wasn't going to be able to go until the swelling in my eyelids went down, so I treated myself to a hot cup of coffee and massaged my eyes with a wet bandanna. The sunrise was brief and glorious.

As if in a dream, I heard a single, brief, melodious birdsong, heralding the sunrise. It was over so quickly I could hardly believe I had heard it, especially since the songster did not repeat himself. Bicknell's thrush? I don't know, maybe.

It was so pure and beautiful- I could hardly believe my ears, but no sooner had I paused to notice the song then it was over. I may never hear it again, but I will never forget it. The song cast a magical spell over the morning. Despite the cold restless night, my troubled vision and worrisome lymph nodes, I felt refreshed and blessed to be alive in such a special place- on Burnt Rock Mountain summit with all of Eastern Vermont spread out below me in the morning light, a glorious song in my ears, the sun already warming my bones, starting a new day, happy to be alive, thankful to be walking on the Long Trail.

The rocks on which I had spent the night were about 500 million or so years old, according to geologists. They were formed from sediment that settled for eons on the bottom of a tropical sea at a time when life did not exist on land, but was starting to blossom into microscopic multicellular replicating organisms in the ocean. The layers of sand, mud and clay accumulated until the chain of islands erupting in the proto-Atlantic ocean "crashed" into North America 354 million years ago, followed by the plate of Africa churning and metamorphosing everything, the equivalent of a geologic train wreck. The sediments were subject to incredible pressures- compressed, squeezed and heated and cooked into new and incredibly hard rock- now the bedrock spine of the Green Mountains. Erosion resistant schist. These rocks had already been formed by the time dinosaurs began to dominate the earth and the first ecosystems developed on land. They still stand high, the topographic backbone of Vermont, while softer rocks around them erode and fill the lowlands with sediment. 500 million years. Even the repeated waves of mile high glaciers that passed over the ridges during the ice ages simply scratched them up a bit manifesting as "glacial striae", like the parallel corduroy grooves on Mansfield's summit ridge. 500 million years. And I had thought that one cold windy night seemed endless. Those rocks were durable and enduring- I was soft, fragile, fleeting, not even a flash in the pan. Not even a speck. One night in that environment had left me blind and vulnerable, but those rocks were barely dented by millenniums of rain, snow, ice, wind or sun. Plants came, germinated, clung to the rock, survived, reproduced and evolved. Animals and people came and left. The rocks remained. But gradually something would change, maybe in another 500 million years, and they would wear down or get folded up again into the earth's crust. Recycled. Nothing lasts for eternity.

My parents had promised each other that they would be together forever. I heard Dad whisper to Mom every night when he left that they would be together in the next world, for eternity. I think the thing that he hated the most about facing death was the fact that he might be separated from my mother. He made me promise that I would put their ashes together and put them in the vault he had bought in the family plot in the cemetery near Philadelphia. So I purchased a double urn made out of the most impervious and durable material I could find. I would have bought a titanium one if I had found it. I chose a brass urn, a heart within a heart with an opening between the two chambers, and had the funeral home mix the ashes together before sealing them in the urn. I figured it would last a long time. Longer than wood or clay. Might even survive an atomic bomb. Might even survive a geologic train wreck, and metamorphose into the backbone of a mountain. I was pretty sure Dad would have approved.

As I sipped coffee and waited for my eyesight to come back I wasn't thinking about plate tectonics. I was thinking about grocery shopping.

Today we are going into Waitsfield! I have been looking forward to Waitsfield because it is the location of Mad River Glen Ski Resort, which is my brother's winter home and the home of his heart, during ski season anyhow. Over the years I have heard a lot about Waitsfield. My dog even wears a collar from Mad River Glen: "Ski it if You Can" it says. Lyssa is the only dog in California with a collar like it and she wears it proudly, but until today she has never actually been to Waitsfield.

This will be my second visit to the town, although in some ways it will feel like a homecoming. When I was still in the R&D ("Research & Development") phase of my hike I flew back to the East Coast to join my brother Dale in taking a look at the lay of the land. I wanted "boots-on-the-ground" intelligence about what I was getting myself- and my fur-ball companions- into. So after work on a Friday evening in July Hank dropped me off at the Sacramento airport and I caught a red-eye to Newark, New Jersey. Dale picked me up at the curb on Saturday morning and we headed North, out of the tangled urban/industrial sprawl of New Jersey, navigating the spiderweb of 12 lane expressways, on-ramps and off-ramps, railroad tracks, canals and bridges, past city skylines, North into New York State, up the Hudson River Valley to Fort Ticonderoga, where we finally headed East into Vermont. Dale had done this pilgrimage hundreds of times of the last 30 years that he had lived and worked in central New Jersey. He spent every winter weekend of his adult life skiing in Vermont. But he had done the trip only in the wintertime- summers were for sailing. This weekend was special though, because Wendy was out of town and he was left to his own devices. There were some hiking trails that he had always wanted to explore that traversed areas where he liked to ski, but he hadn't done them because Wendy wasn't interested and he hardly ever did anything without her. She thought they would be too hard because some of the sections of trail were reputed to be very steep, and there were reports of ropes and ladders along the way. It was the Long Trail. One of the sections Dale proposed to check out was Mount Mansfield and the other was the Monroe Skyline, which is the section from Appalachian Gap to Lincoln Gap. Mad River Glen Ski Area is at the North end of the Monroe Skyline.

The town of Waitsfield lies 8 miles east of Appalachian Gap on Vermont route 17, and is the hometown base for the Mad River Glen Resort as an all-season nexus for outdoor recreational sports enthusiasts. There is an all-purpose outfitter store, a hodge-podge of food stores, restaurants, eateries, coffee shops, inns and lodges. Dale proudly pointed out the existence of a very well stocked hardware store and a library. Being an engineer, Dale believes that hardware stores are more important than grocery stores. He wouldn't have minded living in Waits-field. They spent so much time there during the winter that it might have made sense to have bought a condo or a winter ski lodge home, but instead they had joined the Monmouth County Ski Club which just happened to own a modest lodge at the base of the mountain. Monmouth County is the County in New Jersey in which they lived. The lodge is run as a sort of co-op and Dale and Wendy are members for life. Dale is the guy who fixes anything that needs fixing, makes the coffee in the morning and often shovels the decks and sidewalks. He boasts about being the first one on the mountain in the morning and the last one off it at night. For the last 10 years or so he has been a member of the ski patrol. We had dinner Saturday night at the Mad River Resort Bar & Grill and everyone knew him. Everyone. They asked him about his summer sailing adventures and looked at me side-ways until he introduced me as his sister from California who was coming out to do the Long Trail in September. And then they got all friendly and interested and told me stories about the trail, or about their dogs, or interesting stories about skiing with Dale on the Mountain. I had never seen my brother so at home, or so much a part of a community of peers. He had always been such a nerdy kid- his bedroom had been full of oscilloscopes, radio-parts, and remote-controlled rockets and airplanes. Skiing had always been part of our lives in wintertime growing up in upstate New York, but during college I had lost interest in it. Dale never got tired of skiing however, a passion equally shared by his wife Wendy. It was what they did in the wintertime. Careers and jobs were the means to an end, which was Vermont, skiing. Everyone that I met that evening felt the same way. Skiing was what they did, and Mad River Glen was where they did it. It felt like family even though I was not really a skier anymore. I felt like I belonged. My brother was a member of the Mad River Glen family more than he was a member of the Harman family- I got that- because I was his sister they were polite to me, but because I was a hiker and I was going to do the Long Trail I was accepted into this family of people who loved the Green Mountains of Vermont. No wonder Dale was not particularly enthused about the Sierras and seemed so distant and dis-interested in the trials and tribulations of caring for Dad and Mom. The family of his heart was here in Waitsfield.

I liked Waitsfield too. It had an outdoorsy, liberal environmentalist feeling. I liked much of what I saw in Vermont that weekend. But Dale was right- Waitsfield seemed special. I was looking forward to seeing it again, on foot and up close.

On the trip from Newark airport we crossed into Vermont from New York and proceeded to drive up the valley along the west side of the Green Mountains. In Bristol we turned east again, heading up to Appalachian Gap. On the way up Dale proposed dropping me off at the top of the Gap so that I could do a few miles of trail, southbound, and get a taste of what it was like. Sure! After flying all night and then a six hour car ride the idea of getting out and hiking for a few hours sounded delicious. He would drop me off at the Gap and then drive down to the resort, hike up one of the ski trails and meet me at the Ski Patrol hut at the top of the Double Chair lift. He gave me a map and I hopped out at the top of the pass.

On the north side of the highway there is a large parking area with some interpretive signs. On the south side there is....nothing. I wandered around for 15 minutes looking for the trail. It should be right here, at the top of the Gap. Finally I spotted a rock with white lettering painted on it: LT/SB30'->. The trail was 30 feet to the right of where I had been searching, a narrow chink in the rock sporting a prominent white blaze. My feet were on the Long Trail! Bursting with energy despite the overnight flight and long car ride, I was exhilarated to finally be on the Trail. My legs fairly rejoiced to be stretching out again and I pretty much bounced up the steep ascent of Stark Mountain. I could do this, I decided, even with a full pack. So could Lyssa and Tina. Even when the trail got steeper and rockier I knew that I could manage it. I climbed up several large boulder faces with the iron rungs bolted onto them- no problem. The dogs would be okay too because I knew they would be able to find ways around them through the forest.

Nearer to the top of the ridge the terrain gradually leveled out and I entered the transition zone where broadleaf forest of beech, birch and maple mixes with fir and spruce. I jumped over my first mud puddles and boggy spots and marveled at the thick green carpets of club moss littered with bright white strips of birch bark. I loved it. It was cool, green, wet and full of life! Couldn't be more different than California.

Dale met me at the top of the double chair ski lift, as promised. The hut was not locked, he explained, because hikers were welcome to use it. Especially in the event that someone needed emergency shelter the resort did not want people to have to break into the hut out of desperation. They did request that hikers leave it clean and tidy, however, and he warned me that there was no running water available. Dale felt more than a little possessive

111

about the hut because he spent much of his "on-call" time as a ski patrolman stationed at the hut. It was cozy and had a wonderful picture window overlooking the Mad River Valley far below. He called it his "office", and vastly preferred it to his other office back in the urban jungle of New Jersey. I circled the spot on my map and wrote "okay to stay overnight no water."

There are an awful lot of shelters, lodges and lean-tos along the Long Trail. I guess that would be good if it was really wet and rainy or if you didn't want to carry a tent on your hike. I planned to carry a tent, anticipating that I probably would want to spend my nights away from people, or that I might not be able to make it to the next shelter before darkness fell.

Picking my way down from the summit of Burnt Rock Mountain the morning of September 12, I felt positively celebratory despite the sleepless night, swollen eyelids and tender lymph nodes. I was only 5 miles from the road into Waitsfield and I had options. I like having options. I'd visit the outfitters, the post office and the grocery store. I'd recharge my phone and call my husband who was probably on the verge of hysteria, not having heard from me for several days. I also had the option of spending the night at one of Waitsfield's Inns. The guidebook listed several that were "hiker-friendly" and a few that were even "dog-friendly." I could sleep in a real bed, take a shower, do some laundry. I could find medical help if my eye problem persisted or worsened or if whatever was causing the tenderness in my lymph nodes turned out to be an early symptom of something serious and debilitating.

My brain was buzzing- there was so much to do and so many decisions to make. It would be easy to spend a day or two in Waitsfield, shopping, resting, recharging, getting myself cleaned up and restored. But I wasn't sure about the idea of leaving the trail for awhile. I LIKED being on the trail- it was home. I liked the forest, the trees, the moss, the quiet and solitude, the fresh clean air. Spending the night in a hotel really didn't seem very appealing- closed up in a room would be like being closed up in a box. There would be noises- cars going by, and people talking and thumping around. Then there were the dogs to worry about. I'd need to watch them and make sure they didn't pee or poop on someone's lawn or flower bed, or bring in mud or shed hair all over, or disturb other guests. Ugh. Besides, even if I got cleaned up I'd get dirty and stinky soon enough anyways. I was staying pretty clean as it was, I thought. I took a sponge bath usually every day in a creek and rinsed out my dirty trail clothes pretty often. But the main problem was that my phone was dead and I wouldn't be able to call ahead to see if there was a room available or request transportation. Then I remembered the Double Lift hut: it would be the perfect place to spend the night! I had to get to the trail-head, hitch a ride to Waitsfield and do all of my errands, and then hitch a ride back up to the ski resort and climb 1000'+ up the ski trail with a huge full pack. It was an ambitious plan but if all went well I could do it.

By the time I reached Birch Glen Camp I was feeling better. My eyes seemed fine and my throat hadn't gotten any worse. I had made good time on the easier section of trail and I had a good plan for the day. I tackled the climb up to Molly Stark's balcony like a pro!

Some time later I gratefully descended Baby Stark Mountain, once again feeling profound respect for these Green Mountains and their people. Molly Stark's Balcony- the name invoked an image of a deck or a back porch, maybe complete with French doors, a couple of recliners, a picnic table where you could sit in the shade, admire the view and sip iced tea! Not this Molly Stark. Vermonters are undeniably rugged! The climb got steeper and steeper and ended with a class IV scramble up the backside to the top of a humongous bouldering cliff. Jeez! At least there wasn't a ladder straight up the face!

Luck was with us once we reached the parking area at

Appalachian Gap. Within a few minutes a little blue Toyota RAV4 did a U-turn and pulled up next to us. The driver, a woman who was obviously a dog lover, looked at Lyssa appreciatively. "That's a beautiful shepherd," she said. Yup. "Looks like one I used to have," she added. Then, "I'd love to give you a ride but I don't think I have room." She pointed her thumb at the rear of the RAV, which was stuffed with boxes. I lost no time in shamelessly begging. "We have a really hard time getting a ride," I explained. "We'd appreciate it so much and we really good at cramming ourselves in small places. She can ride on the floor at my feet," I said, pointing at my gorgeous 85 pound lapdog, "and Tina can ride on my lap." "Well, let me see what I can do," she said. YES! I wanted to hug her!

After a few minutes of re-arranging and shuffling things around, Lyssa had her own seat with my pack on the floor at her feet while Tina and I crammed into the front. Our benefactor was a Dairy Herd Health Inspector and the boxes all contained milk samples from dozens of little dairy farms. The samples were on their way to the lab to be checked for signs of inflammation or disease. Suddenly I was plunged into a fascinating free ranging discussion of cows, dairy farming, dogs, the economy and life in upstate rural Vermont for 8 winding miles down the mountain to Waitsfield. My new friend dropped me off at the Outfitters shop on the far side of town. I thanked her profusely, waved good-bye, and turned around to find the store inexplicably closed. It was impossible. I had called them several days before I left California to make sure they would be open and would have the right kind of fuel I needed for my stove. The congenial store owner had even promised to set aside a liter with my name on it under the counter just to be sure! How could he be closed? The sign on the door read: "Family Emergency. Back Thursday." That was it. I didn't have a Plan B. I needed to think. For lack of a better idea I gathered up my things and the girls and reoriented ourselves for the long trudge back towards town. We got as far as the other side of the store when I noticed a car in the driveway. The back door to the building was slightly ajar. Perhaps someone was there who could give me my fuel. I knocked and a woman peeked out the door. She took a look at the dogs- "sorry, we're closed," she said. "But I need my gas," I blurted out. "I'm hiking the Long Trail and I'm out of fuel for my stove and I called a few weeks ago and he said he'd put some aside for me with my name on it and I could get it today." The door cracked open a bit more. "Well, what's your name? I'm just the bookkeeper but I could take a look." "I'm Shirley," I said, "and this is Lyssa and Tina. They're friendly," I added, just in case. The bookkeeper seemed hesitant about the 85 pound shepherd lurking like the big bad wolf on her doorstep. But she offered to let me in, and so I dumped my pack on the porch and tied the girls to it. "Stay," I said, and they both immediately plopped down in the shade next to the pack. Having found the fuel can with my name on it my new friend seemed reassured that I wasn't a tramp or a thief (do they even have those if Vermont?) and asked me if there was anything else I needed. Boy, was there! A headlamp, some rechargeable batteries for my phone, some new clothes and a few good meals! It was a great store; I could have spent the after-noon shopping. But I didn't want to push my luck, so I settled for buying the lightest headlamp I could find and directions to The Hardware Store where I could find my rechargeable batteries. I left the store promising myself I'd return in the not too distant future and do some real shopping- this was my kind of town!

The hardware store was equally accommodating and well-stocked with everything one might wish for. I bought 2 batteries and a small Swiss army knife. The clerk let me plug in my phone under the counter so it would charge up while we went to the nearby Post Office. Life was good.

As in Johnson, there was a steady stream of customers going in and out of the Post Office. The dogs parked themselves on the sidewalk while I rummaged through my resupply box, sorted trash, and repacked all of my gear to make room for the fresh influx of coffee, breakfast bars, tuna, potato soup, dried fruit and snacks. I stuffed Lyssa's packs with 6 more days worth of dog food. A nearby shopkeeper considerately brought the dogs a big bowl of water. An earthy-looking, graying, friendly woman in a comfortable blue dress stopped to admire the dogs and ask me about my trip. After a few minutes she paused and said "would you like to come up to my house and spend the night? I'd really love to hear more about your hike!" I was stunned- and tempted. It was just past noon. I imagined spending the afternoon relaxing on the porch of an old farmhouse, dogs napping contentedly in the shade, talking about life in Vermont, learning about Waitsfield, drinking ice tea and eating a delicious dinner... Maybe there would be a view of the Mountain and we'd be able to get a good perspective of the terrain through which the trail passed. The Trail. I didn't want to be looking at it, I wanted to be ON it! How would I get back to the trail- would she want to give us a ride back up to the Gap at 6 in the morning? Suddenly I could hardly wait to have the Trail under my feet again. It was calling me like a Siren- I wanted to be back in the forest- the cool green stillness with the path winding out before me, following those white blazes, away from the asphalt and hustle and bustle of town. I thanked her profusely and explained that I was compelled to be back on the trail ASAP- I had a tight itinerary and couldn't afford any time off. I was truly and possibly insanely driven. It was a really nice offer and I still regret that I passed it by. It was a road forever not taken. But in that moment it began to become clear to me that being on the trail, in motion, with Lyssa and Tina, was my highest priority at that time. Not just a priority, but it was where I belonged, and where I deeply needed to be. The Trail was calling and Waitsfield would have to wait!

I retrieved my newly resuscitated phone and headed for the edge of town, calling Hank as I went. It was still morning in California, so he hadn't yet had time to work up an anxiety about me. He knew I hadn't been able to call him until I reached Waitsfield and got charged up again, but he was still happy and relieved to know that I was alive and well. I promised to call him later that evening from the Double Lift Hut and ended the call when a pick-up truck pulled over to the shoulder to give us a lift. It was a carpenter from the ski resort. I had seen him at the Post Office. A friend of my brother Dale, he had to pick us up!

I was more than grateful not to have to walk up the busy narrow curvy highway with the dogs. It was a long 3 or 4 miles up to the ski area and my pack weighed a ton. With the help of my guardian angels, both seen and unseen, I had accomplished all of my errands in remarkably good time. Even so, I barely made it up to the hut by sunset. The ski trail I labored up was unrelentingly vertical. I zig-zagged up, climbing steadily. Shifting into trudge mode, I took baby steps and paced myself according to what my legs were able to maintain without becoming exhausted. The mind focuses, slow and steady. It's the Zen of climbing. All anxieties and mental turmoils subside and fade away as the world morphs and contracts down to the simple act of placing the foot forward, or sideward, but always upward of where it was, placing the pole, balancing and moving again, ever closer to the top. I am goal oriented, for sure, but this was more than a compulsion to reach a goal. This was peace of mind; freedom from everyday worries and demands. Perhaps this serenity was what I craved when I felt so desperate to get back to the Trail. Maybe this was like being an addict, craving the attainment of some altered state. I'm addicted to serenity and the Trail is my drug of choice. I don't know, and it doesn't matter. Nothing matters except taking the step. With each step the view is incrementally better and I am incrementally closer to the Double Lift Hut.

When I finally reached the hut I gratefully dumped my pack on the porch, and then relieved Lyssa of hers. The girls looked at me expectantly- it was dinner time. Digging out their dishes and rations I realized that I had forgotten about water. "Crap," I said. There had been several

tiny little streamlets a ways back down. We'd have to go down and find one. So that was what we did. Gathered up the water containers and headed back down the hill. A few hundred feet down I found a tiny spring running out of the hillside next to the trail- just enough to scoop up clean water to fill the bottles. Then back up we went, still trudging, but arriving in time to watch the sunset fading into night and the twinkling lights of the Mad River Valley coming alive far, far below. This must be how the earth looks from heaven, I thought. The world doesn't get any prettier.

I sat at the window eating soup and dried fruit, soaking up the warm summer evening, feeling very much at peace. I could hardly believe that only twelve hours ago I was waking up on the summit of Burnt Rock Mountain. The day had been so full. I hadn't stopped moving or pushing for an instant, until now. I had a leisurely talk with Hank and then wrote a few lines in the guest book, thinking that Dale or Wendy would find them in a few months when the world would be white and frozen. How glad I was to be there in September when the hills were

green and lush, with just a hint of fall color. How glad I was to be there.

Chapter 6

September 13, 2016

Day 11
Monroe Skyline

If I had to choose my most favorite section of Trail, Monroe Skyline from App Gap to Lincoln Gap might be top of the list. I confess, I'm partial to ridge-lines. A nice open ridge is as close as you can come to flying without an airplane, with your feet on the ground and sky all around you. Of course Monroe Skyline is forested, but there are views at the ski areas and a spectacular, rare 360 degree view at the top of Mount Abraham. Plus I was still riding high on my elation that we have made it past the Rump and the dreaded silver ladder, and had a good night's sleep in the Double Hut as a bonus.

We left the Hut as the sun was just peeking over the eastern horizon. Feeling invincible, Lyssa and Tina and I tore up the trail to the lofty summit of the Mad River Glen Ski area, the lodge known as the Stark's Nest, located at the top of the resort's famous antique single chair lift. The lodge is open to hikers and was occupied that morning by 3 slumbering, snoring backpackers. But not for long. Lyssa was ecstatic to discover once again her old friends from the lean-to on Bamforth Ridge and she lost no time in joyously rousting them out of their cocoons. Fortunately they were delighted to see her also, and insisted they had been just about to get up anyhow. I was about to leave them to their morning but my phone rang as I was hoisting my pack- Dale and Wendy were calling from their boat somewhere on the Chesapeake Bay. By way of an unseen array of towers, satellites and a large bit of what, from my perspective, could have only been magic, I could hear the breeze rattling the halyards against the mast. Dale had rigged up a hot-spot and plugged it into the sound system of their sailboat. He promised to meet me at the end of the trail at the Pine Mountain trail-head on September 23rd, or wherever I might end up being on that day at 5:00 in the afternoon. He still wasn't convinced that I would make it the whole way. Neither was I. I only knew that today would be a great day doing the ridge, and by nightfall we would be in the Breadloaf Mountains, back in the wilderness.

Skiing was brought to the United States by Scandinavian immigrants and had been a Thing in this country for at least a century before it became an industry. The first mechanical lift, a rope tow rigged up with the engine of a model T truck, was invented in Vermont in 1934. Stowe, Smuggler's Notch , Big Bromley and Pico Peak were founded in the 30's. But the industry really got rolling in the 1950s, after World War II, when Americans once again had time and resources for outdoor recreation. Development was so rapid and uncontrolled that for awhile it seemed like the Long Trail was in danger of being literally overrun by commercial development. Fortunately for tree-huggers like me, enough people in Vermont had enough sense to recognize the value of preserving the state's mountains and forests and wilderness areas, and were actually able to effect the passage of legislation to protect it. In 1970 a law was passed curtailing development above 2'500 feet elevation. This amazing piece of legislation, known as Act 250, has been an invaluable tool for the environmental conservation community, led by the Green Mountain Club, to keep the Wild in the Wilderness. I tromped along the Monroe Skyline in blissful ignorance of the political forces that had shaped the very trail under my feet; the rocky ridge is thickly forested,

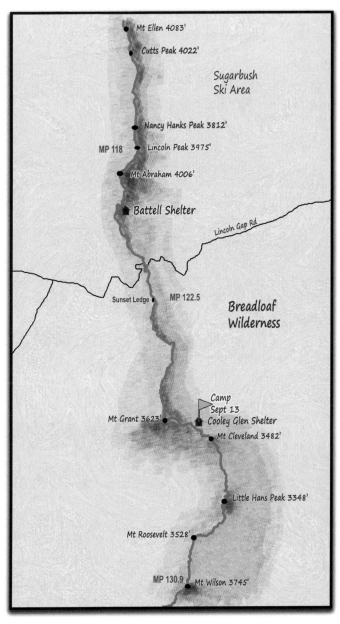

Mt Ellen 4083'

Cutts Peak 4022'

Sugarbush
Ski Area

Nancy Hanks Peak 3812'

MP 118   Lincoln Peak 3975'

Mt Abraham 4006'

Battell Shelter

Lincoln Gap Rd

Sunset Ledge   MP 122.5

Breadloaf
Wilderness

Camp
Sept 13
Cooley Glen Shelter

Mt Grant 3623'

Mt Cleveland 3482'

Little Hans Peak 3348'

Mt Roosevelt 3528'

MP 130.9   Mt Wilson 3745'

Map 7: The Monroe Skyline and the Breadloaf Wilderness

interrupted periodically with a break for a ski trail, lift terminal, seasonal lodge facility or overlook. I knew nothing of the years of lobbying, negotiating, marketing and campaigning, the dedicated and sustained efforts and outreach and education that had gone into preserving the mountain ecosystem, ultimately resulting in a partnership with the ski industry to find ways to save the mountains for the benefit of both hikers and skiers. I just knew that I loved the trail, loved being there and I loved Vermont for having this trail and these mountains. I didn't know how lucky we are to have the trail the way it is, how in the 1930s there was a proposal to build a parkway along the whole length of the summit ridge of the Green Mountains, which was fought off in part by the Green Mountain Club and their campaign to convince the people of Vermont to value the wilderness character of their land. Vermont is green and lovely, with a clean, unspoiled, pastoral landscape. The state speed limit is 50 mph, there are only 2 interstates and billboards are illegal. The conservation community is strong and robust. But the pressures on the land are constant and relentless too, especially from off-road-vehicle users and timber companies. Vandalism is a constant problem at any of the huts and lean-tos situated within a mile or two of road access. It's a constant push/pull, yin and yang. The Long Trail is the oldest long distance backpacking trail in the United States, founded as a "footpath in the wilderness." But the miracle of the Long Trail is that it is so much more than a dirt track 10 inches wide and 273 miles long- it is the State Treasure of Vermont. It is loved and cherished and is a source of pride for thousands of Vermonters and this huge community of people who have grown up around it, maintaining it, protecting it, promoting it, hiking on it and loving it. Every Vermonter I met knows about and takes pride in the Long Trail, whether they have ever hiked it or not. I met shopkeepers who had been born and raised in Vermont and had never set foot on the Trail but were proud of it nevertheless. It's amazing to me to discover a society where land conservation is a common social value. Such is not the case in the rural northern sierra foothill county where I live, where environmentalists are derided and railed against. Vermont's land ethic is seems precious and fragile. I walked along above the ski

Quad Chairlift

resorts, looking down on the roads, parking lots, lodges, and lift towers and terminals far below. I emerged from cool green moist alpine woodland onto the mown weed-stubble sun baked ski trails and was relieved and grateful when the trail re-entered the shady refuge of the forest.

Mount Ellen, Castle Rock, Lincoln Peak, and then Mount Abraham, which is above tree-line and has a marvelous view- on a clear day you can pick out the Adirondacks of New York and the White Mountains over in New Hampshire. When Dale and I did the ridge-line in July we were greeted by the GMC caretaker on Mount Abraham summit. I had quizzed him thoroughly for

Athos, Porthos, Aramis and Lyssa

information about the trail and promised I'd see him in September, so I was disappointed that he was not at his summit station to meet Lyssa and Tina and see that we had made it. The GMC caretakers are Guardians of the Wilderness- real superheros. I wish I could have been one. But today I am just an unremarkable middle aged lady from California, passing through. Here today, gone tomorrow. With 2 very remarkable 4 footed companions. Runaways from the west coast. Catch us if you can.

Still feeling elation at having made it past Mansfield, The Camels Hump, Ladder Gap and the Stark Mountains, I was almost skipping on the way down to Lincoln Gap from Mount Abraham, when I met the nearly naked man. Wearing nothing except a scanty pair of black trunks, he was climbing up the rocky ravine below me. Lean and lithe, toes curling around the footholds, arms waving free for balance, he appeared to be dancing up the mountain, as light as air. I stopped and blinked to clear my vision, and he smiled at me. "Wow," was all that I could say. Another smile. He floated up past me and I took a few steps down the mountain. Then I stopped and turned around to double check and make sure he was not a hallucination. As if he knew I was looking he turned around and smiled at me again. I sort of waved a lame salute and we continued on our respective ways. My high tech hyperlight pack never felt so heavy as it did that moment. Oh, to be so unburdened and travel so lightly through life. What had he sacrificed to be so free, was it worth it? I wondered. Well, I'm probably carrying a lot more burdens in life than I need to these days. Surely I can shed a few things, starting with all that old furniture out in the garage! Maybe I can learn something from this man.... Here's a thought- maybe it's not so much that the furniture itself is heavy, but it's all of the invisible sentiment and memories that are attached to it that makes it so weighty and cumbersome to deal with. If I let go of the furniture what will happen to the memories? Would I offend Mom's ghost if I donate her favorite chair to the thrift store? Am I ready to find out? Answer- I'm getting readier with every step! Southbound, we roll!

Around 1:00 we crossed the Lincoln Gap Road, hurrying across to enter the Breadloaf Mountains. We don't stop until we are well away from the road, once again in the embrace of the forest. In the Wilderness.

At Lincoln Gap we hit the lowest elevation of the day- 2,424 feet. For the next four and a half miles to Cooley Glen we would be climbing again, a slow steady ascent of 1,200 feet to the summit of Mount Grant before dropping down to the shelter. We had already clicked off a respectable 10 mile chunk of trail and it was still only mid-day, so I wasn't worried about another almost 5 miles. But my going-up muscles, which had taking it pretty easy all day, were not happy about changing gears, and suddenly my pace slowed to a crawl again. My energy flagged in the afternoon heat and my pack felt heavier and heavier with each step up in elevation. At Sunset Ledge we stopped to rest and enjoy the view. I could see what I thought must be Mount Grant- it looked very far away. The map said 2.8 miles. Three hours later I was still climbing. Vermont miles. Don't underestimate them! At the summit I found a good cell signal and stopped to call Hank for the first and only time all day. The day was sliding into evening; already the light was softening and the temperature had dropped enough that I began to feel a bit of chill as I sat on the highest point I could find, trying to give my poor lonely spouse a few moments of wifely attention. But all too soon my leg muscles started to stiffen up and I got nervous about descending Mount Grant in the fading light. Cooley Glen was on the shady side of the ridge and it looked a lot darker down there than I would have expected. Of course, we were in the thick spruces again instead of the open airy broad-leaf forest we'd traveled through for most of the way up the ridge. I flew as fast as I could down the mountain, but even so it seemed like a long eight tenths of a mile until we finally strode into Cooley Glen. One reason the light had faded so quickly into dimness was because a cloud-bank had moved in during the late afternoon and the forecast was calling for a chance of rain starting that night and continuing for the next few days. At the shelter we were greeted by a young woman and her dog- wow, another female hiking with a canine companion!- I wanted to talk dogs and hiking with her but her dog, a high strung border collie, was terrified of Lyssa and barked her head off if we came anywhere close. Lyssa ignored her and Tina gave them a wide berth. I asked the young lady where the water source was and she waved vaguely off towards the south. I barely had time to find the spring 100 yards down a side trail and make it back to the lean-to when the last bit of light disappeared.

Cooley Glen was not an inviting place to spend time, but I was exhausted and it was dark, so I was pretty much stuck there. It was gloomy. The air felt damp and muggy and filled with the odor of an old stinky fire pit. The border collie and her human companion were tenting, so to save time I decided to stake my claim in the unoccupied lean-to. I wouldn't have to worry about potential rain, and with Lyssa and Tina nearby I wouldn't have to worry about the mice who regularly resided in all of the shelters along the trail. I must have slept some, but mostly I tossed and turned and listened to the night. As in the other shelters, the hollow raised floor acted like a resophonic amplifier. Every scrape and rustle of nylon echoed in my ears, along with the steady washing-machine slosh of Tina's dysplastic heart valves. Lyssa barked once during the night- probably the border collie- woman was out tending to business. My mind was racing with trail math- how many miles left to go to the southern terminus and how many days did I have to get there. It was the night of September 13th and I had 146 miles to go to the Southern Terminus. Dale was picking me up on the 23rd. I had to average at least 15 miles a day in order to make it on time. That was do-able, but the problem was the mail drops. When I first plotted out my hike, I had figured on finishing on the 25th, which gave me two extra days to play with. Two extra days to go the miles, but also two extra days worth of food to pack and carry. To be on the safe side I had arranged an extra mail drop for the remaining section of the trail- one in Killington and one in Manchester Center. Even if I could have pushed myself harder than I was now, (which probably was not even an option,) I didn't see how I would be able to do both mail-drops and still have enough time to complete the trail. If only I could figure out a way to eliminate the Manchester re-supply, I thought. It might be possible, but I'd still have to push myself. I didn't give a thought to any alternative ideas such as quitting early and taking a few days off for R&R at some scenic resort, or having Dale pick me up a week early and go down to his house in New Jersey to visit and rest. I could have even gotten off the trail at any of the road crossings and hired transportation to take me back up to Troy to retrieve my car and then take my time driving back to California, and maybe stop and do a little sight-seeing along the way. None of those ideas held any appeal. I was becoming obsessed with finishing the Trail.

If only I could find a way to travel as lightly as the near-ly-naked man I saw on Mount Abraham, I thought. I could spend the rest of my days wandering the Earth freely, without encumbrance or constraint. How wonderful that would be. How could such a thing be possible? Did the man have a home base, in Waitsfield perhaps. Was he a monk, was there a monastery here in the Green Moun-tains? I couldn't imagine me living an ascetic lifestyle, but I had to find a way to simplify my life and shed some of my burdens. We could move to a smaller house, a cabin would be fine. One story, nothing fancy, with a garden, a little workshop. And wifi, of course. There had to be a way to get away from my responsibilities and obligations. I needed to reduce all the stress in my life. The answer was out there. The nearly-naked man was a messenger, if only I could figure out the message. He'd smiled at me- I must be doing something right- but his eyes were dark and mysterious; was he laughing at my folly and self delusion? On top of everything there was the question I'd been denying and ducking for years: what about Hank. How would a quest to simplify life and lighten my load affect my marriage? Something had to change. I had 10 more days to find the answer, and I'd have to work for it. Somehow finishing the trail and reclaiming my life were becoming intertwined, as if by proving that I was strong enough to do the first, I would be able to accomplish the second. I could do it, but only by taking one step at a time. It was a long night.

September 14, 2016

Day 12
Cooley Glen to Sucker Brook

The approaching change in the weather, portending the potential for rain, lent a restless, PMS-type feeling to the night at Cooley Glen Shelter. In the morning the smokey gloom and an overly full privy inspired me to get an early start. Being on the Trail, in motion, constantly in the moment of one step ahead of where I'd been and one step away from where I would be next, felt comfortable, and right. There's magic in mists. The hush that falls over a forest in a mist is more than absence of sound- it's a palpable and tactile feeling that you can touch with your ears. You can close your eyes and feel the hush with your skin. Everything is still. The Breadloaf Mountains are a cloud forest, wet, dripping, hidden and still. An in-between world, dream-like. I like it. It doesn't matter whether we are going up or down; it's all the same. Time and motion are meaningless abstractions- it's always here and now. Now we are here, at the Burnt Hill trail intersection, the official halfway milepost of the Long Trail. Now we are here, crossing Highway 125. A skinny woman wearing purple shorts, running shoes, and a big backpack, accompanied by a giant black and tan dog who looks like a wolf except she's also wearing a backpack, and a little feathery brown pup, who looks like a dancing fox and is not wearing anything; we appear to startle the road crew workers lounging on their backhoes, and then we disappear. At dusk we reappear at Sucker Brook Shelter, and camp for the night. Southbound!

It was still pitch black dark in Cooley Glen when my alarm went off at 5:30 in the morning. It hadn't rained during the night and the air was practically edematous with moisture. I shoved my feet into my shoes and made a dash for the privy. Or at least, I tried to. Border collie woman had pitched her tent right in the middle of the path from the lean-to to the outhouse, and so I detoured way around her to avoid disturbing her and ended up missing the outhouse altogether and nearly getting lost in the dark, smothering damp gloomy woods. Tripping over logs and brush, I finally nearly crashed into the tent. Collie girl was up. "Oh, I'm sorry, I can't find the outhouse," I apologized as she awkwardly hung onto her frantic barking dog. She pointed her headlamp behind the tent- the privy was right there. "Oh, Thank God!" I apologized again for the disturbance and dashed for the privy. It was nearly full. Of human waste. There was maybe 3 inches of space between the seat and the top of the pile, and even less than that by the time I was done. Obviously there was no caretaker on duty to deal with the situation. Feeling somewhat guilty for having contributed to making a bad situation even worse, I hurried to finish my business and get the hell out of there. Collie girl was already striking her tent and stuffing things into her pack. We gave her a wide berth going back to the lean-to. A few minutes later she appeared, fully packed and ready to go.

"Have a good hike," she said. I asked her about her plans for the day, thinking she might be interested in knowing about the Double Lift Hut. "Oh, I'm going to take it easy and just go to Battell Shelter today," she said. "I'm worried about the rain. And, besides, I did an 18 mile day yesterday, which was really a lot, for me," she added. I asked her where she had camped the previous night to have hiked such a long way. "Sucker Brook Shelter," she said. "But it was probably harder than it needed to be because I missed a few turns." The border collie, wearing a sleek red light-weight looking pack, was bouncing up and down next to her. "Well, have a good hike," she repeated, striding off up the trail. "Have a good hike," I said. I watched the dog capering along happily by her side. I was only a little envious- at least she'd be able to carry the her up and down the ladders.

A short while later I was ready to go too. Even without the chore of striking and stowing the tent, it still took me awhile to feed Lyssa and Tina, measure out my rations for the day, and figure out my strategy for dealing with a possible day of hiking in the rain. All of my gear, including my cell phone and maps, had to be protected from wetness. I needed to stay dry too, but I knew I would get hot if I started out with too many layers of clothing, so I ended up wearing shorts and tank top underneath my rain pants and shell. I was eager to get started because I had hopes of reaching Sucker Brook Shelter by nightfall. If I could, I would try to repeat Collie Girl's 18 mile day feat in reverse. Already I was wasting precious daylight!

I don't think it ever actually rained that day, but it was wet enough walking through the clouds of mist drifting through the trees, shrouding the hills and valleys and obscuring the views. It was easy to stay in the moment of walking, walking, walking, with nothing to see but white mist and green forest. The world was quiet and featureless. We only met a few other hikers, appearing by surprise out of the mists and then quickly disappearing. Cell signals were few and far between- I sent a few texts to Hank when I could, and maybe I got a few back. It didn't matter. I had breakfast and coffee at Emily Proctor. At Boyce Shelter I met a young woman backpacker from New Zealand. Intrigued by how she had come to be hiking on the Long Trail of Vermont, I engaged her in talking about her world wandering journey while I shared a bag of tuna with Lyssa and Tina. The clouds seemed to be lifting and so I peeled off the rain gear before resuming. A half mile later I arrived at the Burnt Hill Trail intersection: "Halfway," I told the girls, and slapped the top of

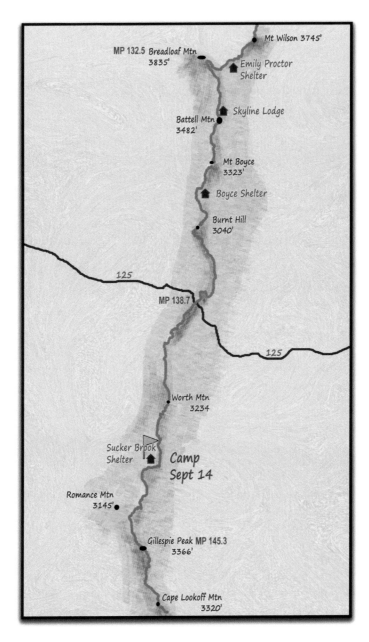

Mt Wilson 3745'

MP 132.5 Breadloaf Mtn
3835'

Emily Proctor
Shelter

Skyline Lodge

Battell Mtn
3482'

Mt Boyce
3323'

Boyce Shelter

Burnt Hill
3040'

125

MP 138.7

125

Worth Mtn
3234

Sucker Brook
Shelter

Camp
Sept 14

Romance Mtn
3145'

Gillespie Peak MP 145.3
3366'

Cape Lookoff Mtn
3320'

Map 8: Breadloaf Mtn to Sucker Brook Shelter

the signpost. An hour later we were out of the Breadloaf Wilderness, crossing highway 125. Striding purposefully, still on a mission.

It was early in the afternoon and I only had 4.6 miles to go to reach Sucker Brook Shelter. But just like yesterday I was facing nearly 1,200 feet of uphill climbing and starting to feel tired from the hours of walking. It's okay if I don't make it, I told myself. I could just go a couple more miles and I'd have my 15 mile quota. I could camp anywhere along the way. There was only one problem with that plan: water. Walking through mist and clouds for most of the day, I had lowered my guard about planning ahead for water sources. The only water source shown on the map between highway 125 and Sucker Brook Shelter is Lake Pleiads, at the base of Middlebury Snow Bowl ski resort and at the bottom of the big ascent. I didn't want to camp near the lake, but neither did I want to fill up the water containers to lug up the mountain for the three of us to dry camp that night. I checked the time and decided that we should be able to make it to Sucker Brook before dark.

The initial ascent up the Middlebury Ski bowl was steep and hard. Just like yesterday my tired legs protested painfully each step up, and my pace slowed to a crawl. "Shouldn't I be getting used to this?" I thought, pushing myself. My legs screamed back. "Why, why, why are we doing this again," they said. The endless uphill creep ended when we reached the border of the Joseph Battell Wilderness. Joseph Battell, a 19th century millionaire from Middlebury who bought Camel's Hump Mountain and gave it, along with the surrounding land, to the State of Vermont in 1911. My kind of millionaire. Ah, wilderness- a salute to Mr Battell. We were still going uphill, but the grade lessened, and by 4:30 we reached the top of Worth Mountain. I hugged my girls. "We're gonna make it!" I told them. And we did. 1 hour and 1.8 long Vermont miles later we arrived, grateful and exhausted, at Sucker Brook Shelter. A handful of campers were puttering around in and around the lean-to, reading, resting, pumping water and messing with their gear. It was easy to find

a nice tent-site not too far from a tiny brooklet; Lyssa and Tina availed themselves of the fresh clear water and then flopped down next to my pack, barely stirring enough to eat their dinner rations. I ate my soup, studied the map and did the math. We'd come 17.1 miles, but then, we hadn't gotten lost or taken any wrong turns. Other than the two stops for coffee and lunch with the New Zealander, we hadn't stopped moving all day. I was proud of having done 17 miles, our best day yet with a full pack and lots of up and down, but I was totally exhausted. Shouldn't I be getting in shape and getting used to this by now? Wasn't it supposed to start getting easier now that we were officially through with the rugged north? Would I be able to do 9 more days like this? There was only one way to find out. I was on a mission. I studied guidebook and the map, and re- ran the numbers in my mind while organizing my gear for a quick and early departure in the morning. It was 15 miles to Telephone Gap- that was my minimum. The next shelter after that, Ralston Rest, was at the 20 mile mark for the day- probably too much. Was there water in between? I squinted at the map- there was a faint blue line near the trail at the base of Dave's Peak, but would it have water? Should I take the chance?
I set my alarm for 5 am and surrendered to the night. Tomorrow would be here all too soon- it was time to rest.

Somehow the journey was truly beginning to change who I was. I felt like I was in a crucible, being reformed, reworked, strengthened and hardened into something new. Something free and better; finishing the Trail was an important part of the realization of that process. Obsession with the goal of hiking the entire length of the Long Trail was slowly infiltrating my consciousness, replacing my prior endless and fruitless obsession with re-living my parents' last few difficult years, and wondering what I could have done differently, or better. I was escaping a mind-trap, an infinite maze with no way out. I had been stuck in a neural loop with a synaptic misfire, but now the loop was crumbling. In it's place was the Long Trail, emerging. Later I came to see The Long Trail as merely

133

the beginning of an altogether new trail, like a wormhole or bridge into an entirely different life path. The new trail would be all my own to choose and follow. It was a rebirth and birthing is never easy, or painless. To get to the other side I had to travel a one hundred and thirty mile birth canal in 9 days! One day at a time. One step at a time.

Chapter 7

September 15, 2016

Day 13
Porcupines

I was ready to hit the trail just as it was getting light enough to see, and headed for the path leading from the shelter area to the main trail. As we passed the lean-to a tousled head popped up from the mass of sleeping bags and I clicked my tongue to Lyssa so that she wouldn't decide to detour over there and rouse everyone out of bed. It's her self-appointed duty to welcome slumbering humans into a joyful new day. "Getting an early start," said the head. I waved and called to Lyssa again. Both dogs were bright and perky, as if the marathon of the previous day had been completely forgotten. Cool! I felt pretty good too. We were off.

The first few miles out of Sucker Brook wind through lovely open broad-leaf forest. First comes Romance Gap, a name which inspires fantasies of lovers meeting secretly in the forest. I wondered what might have become of them, but they had left no clue, no trace. Only a winding path. Then Gillespie Peak, which I imagined must have been named after an early trail blazer, or perhaps his little brother. I stopped at the summit marker and brewed

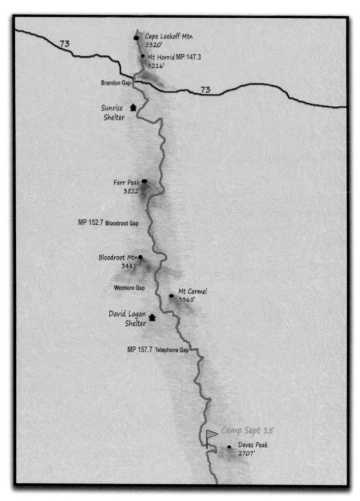

Map 9: *Mt Horrid, Sunrise Shelter, Bloodroot Gap Telephone Gap, and Dave's Peak*

a cup of coffee for second breakfast. Gillespie's coffee shop, I thought. The coffee re-energized me for the next mile and a half of down/up to the summit of Cape Lookoff Mountain, which makes me think of my brothers and their boats. They had their lookouts, I had mine. I had no wish to trade places.

Next came a 1 mile dipsy doodle, Mt Horrid, another imagination-stimulating name. The best I could come up with was the feeble observation that the cone shaped summit looked sort of like a witch's pointy hat, but then I think I read that it was named after some notable person. Mount Horrid and Mount Horrid's Great Cliff, which were highly recommended side trip, but my inner slave-driver did the math and told me I must press onward if I wanted to make my 15+ miles before dark. I'll come back and do them later, I thought. Someday. We continued on, tumbling down the mountain to Brandon Gap at highway 73. 5 miles down, 12 more to go, more or less.

At the parking lot on the south side of the road I met 3 trail caretakers getting ready to head out to Sunrise Shelter- their mission: retire the current privy and create a new one. Wow! The leader was a young woman who was the maintenance coordinator for that who section of trail. I mentioned the unfortunate condition of the revolting overly full privy at Cooley Glen and she made a note in her notebook. "We'll take care of it," she said. I was curious about the technique for retiring an outhouse, and quizzed the crew on the way up the trail. They were lugging a heavy load of pine shavings, shovels and rakes. I had to double my usual plodding-along pace to keep up with them. It was amazing to me that the Green Mountain Club was able to come up with the funds to pay these young people to work so hard to keep the trail clean and pristine, to lug these heavy loads of tools and supplies for miles into the forest to deal with human waste. I felt immensely grateful to them, and told them so. There is nothing worse than finding human waste near some beautiful back country camping spot. Wisps of toilet paper poking

up from the soil or clinging to the brush like prayer flags brings out homicidal urges in me. I wished I was 40 years younger so that I could be a GMC trail caretaker. I'd have to settle for making a donation instead. Puncheons and Privies!

Looking ahead at the next 12 miles of trail there were no apparent water sources shown on the map. However there had been a half dozen or so minor creek crossings between highway 73 and Sunrise Shelter, so I had to believe that there would be some water along the way. I filled up the water bags just in case, and put a couple of partially filled bottles in Lyssa's saddlebags. It was a smart move.

At Sunrise Shelter I parted ways with my caretaker

Lyssa on the trail to Bloodroot Gap

friends, grateful to be hiking on instead of digging an outhouse. I was also glad to resume my usual more slow and steady pace for the next 3.3 (Vermont) miles of gradual uphill. The grade was so gradual it was hardly noticeable. In fact, the whole leg up to Bloodroot Gap would have been pretty much unmemorable except for Lyssa. I probably should have put her on a leash when I read the notice about the porcupines. Somewhere between the Chittenden Brook Trail junction and Farr Peak Lyssa suddenly charged off into the forest and disappeared.

In 5 years of hiking together Lyssa had rarely disappeared. Usually it was after a deer or jackrabbit who had easily left her far behind. I didn't know what she would do if she ever caught anything or encountered something truly dangerous, like a bear or a mountain lion. She liked to chase things but she didn't seem to have a killer instinct, plus she was pretty smart. There was one time she happened to catch a fat young marmot. She seemed more surprised than anything when she brought it to show me. It was screaming it's head off and when I made her drop it waddled off into the bush apparently unharmed. The first time she met a small herd of cows grazing near the trail she was mostly curious and sort of bouncedaround them playfully until a Mama cow put her head down and charged at her. Lyssa hightailed it back to the trail and put me between her and cows for the rest of the trip. Smart. I figured she'd be equally cautious around a moose. But I wouldn't put it past her to try to pick up a porcupine, if only just once.

In the past Lyssa always found her way back to me, but only after too many long heart-wrenching minutes of suppressed panic on my part. Usually by the time she trotted back to me, grinning and panting her head off, I'd be hoarse from bellowing. I hated it. The last time she did it was on the PCT near Ebbet's Pass, and when she returned one of her packsaddle bags was torn loose and hanging by a thread. I had a sewing kit and spent the next hour repairing it. Darn dog. All I could do was bellow her name as loud as I could and keep walking. After 5 or 10 minutes that seemed like an hour I heard her coming up behind me like a freight train. Fast, and not slowing down. As she tore by at 90 miles an hour I saw white things sticking out of the end of her muzzle. Quills.

Working at the emergency clinic in the rural Sierra foothills I had treated a number of dogs for porcupine encounters. Mostly pitbulls. Pits were notorious for getting quilled, probably because they didn't have the sense to let go. Some pits were frequent customers at the clinic. Treatment required general anesthesia and a good pair of pliers.

Lyssa flew by pretty fast but it looked like there were only a few quills, mostly in the tip of her nose. I called her back to me and lassoed her with the leash. She was beside herself with excitement but she didn't seem to be in distress otherwise. I think she was in too much of a frenzy to feel the quills stuck in her nose. I put her in a headlock and yanked the quills out as fast as I could, one by one. She didn't like it. By the seventh quill I couldn't hold her any longer but I was done. We dodged the bullet, but had she learned her lesson? Who knows? I kept her on leash most of the rest of the day. Porcupines!

Bloodroot Gap was unremarkable despite it's ominous name. Bloodroots are actually a type of wildflower, but I didn't see any of those either. The next few miles were downhill and we made good time to the intersection with the trail leading down to David Logan shelter. By then I had gotten in the habit of asking everyone I me for information on water sources, and I knew that David Logan Shelter had no water. No one could remember if there was water between here and Ralston Rest, 7.7 miles away. I didn't think we could make it to Ralston before dark. Surprisingly there was cell service at the junction and I was able to send a quick check-in text to Hank. He was alarmed about the porcupine but by then I was more worried about finding water and a place to camp, so I cut it short and hurried on.

At 4:30 we reached Telephone Gap. There was a tiny rivulet dribbling down the rock and no likely places to camp. I had another 2 hours of daylight and the map showed a couple of more promising blue squiggles intersecting the trail about 2 miles ahead. It was worth a chance and we hurried on. At 6:00 I found a tiny stream near the base of Dave's Peak; the headwaters of Jimmy Dean Brook. It was shallow and kind of swampy in spots, but it was flowing and the girls had no trouble lapping it up. It was easy to find a nice clean flat spot well away from the trail, and in no time we were home for the night. The forest quickly grew dark and there was no sound. Tina and Lyssa settled down close by and I gratefully collapsed in my sleeping bag. By headlamp I did the math- 17 miles! Tomorrow I could easily make it to Killington- a day early!- and pick up my mail drop. The plan was working! I had a chance of finishing the trail! I turned out the light and just for the heck of it I turned on the phone to check for a cell signal. To my utter surprise there was a LTE service. How it penetrated that deep dark thick silent forest I do not know, but I called Hank. He answered and for the first time in days we were able to have a pleasant unhurried conversation. He found Dave's Peak on the map, found the horseshoe bend in the trail, and found the little blue thread where we were camped. It was the next best thing to being there. We talked about porcupines, mileage, water, and whether or not I might finish the trail, and he filled me in on things at home, which were pretty uneventful. I slept like a log and didn't wake up once all night long.

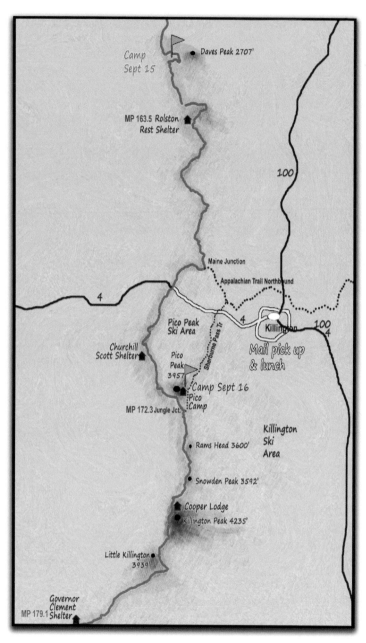

Map 10 Maine Junction, Killington, Pico Peak

September 16, 2016

Day 14
Killington

I wish I could say that every night on the trail was spent in such profoundly peaceful, uninterrupted slumber. In truth most nights were comprised of a series of naps interspersed with periods of tossing and turning and mental churning. Recently, out of necessity, the churning had changed in character: instead of obsessively re-living my mother's death I thought about the Trail and the challenges of the day ahead. It was a relief not to be stuck in a Sisyphean dead-end canyon anymore.

Today's challenge was the Killington mail-drop, specifically getting from the trail-head at the Highway 4 intersection down the road to the Killington Post Office, which was 2.4 miles of busy highway. Specifically, getting down it with 2 dogs.

Before I reached Highway 4 I would come to a major milestone known as the Maine Junction, where the Long Trail meets the Appalachian Trail. From that point south to near the Massachusetts state line the Long Trail and the Appalachian Trail were one in the same trail- the route was shared. It was the LT/AT, or Long Trail/ Appalachian Trail. The north bound hikers I would meet might be heading for Canada via the Long Trail, or they might be AT hikers heading for Maine via the AT. For north-bounders the split occurred at Maine Junction. It sounds simple enough, but it gets confusing because after splitting off from the conjoined LT/AT, the AT headed east for awhile and then actually veered south again before correcting its course to head up northeast to Maine. If your still with me this far, good. There's another twist. About 2.3 miles from Maine Junction the northbound AT intersects Vt Highway 100 only 0.4 miles from the Killington Post Of-

143

fice! So if I went that way I would only have to deal with 0.4 miles of road walking versus 2.4 miles on Highway 4 if I stayed on the Long Trail.

I puzzled over this tangled web for a long time. It continually confused me that the AT northbound would actually take me to Killington, which was to the southeast of the junction. In the end I couldn't get past this contradiction and I chose to remain on the Long Trail and take my chances on getting a ride. I was a LT hiker, not an AT hiker. I would stay faithful to my path, the Trail that had become my home. I loved the Long Trail. In my mind she was personified as a tough, playful spirit, a minor goddess in Mother Nature's pantheon. I wanted to do every step and join the ranks of the end-to-enders club. Besides, it just made life simpler to stick to one trail.

The thing about a solo backpacking trip (not counting canine companions) is that you have to make all your own decisions, and you are the only person to blame for the consequences. I always wondered how the day would have gone if I had chosen to turn left at Maine Junction and followed the AT north down to Killington. Followed a different path, met different people. Good things happened that might not have happened, bad things that I might have avoided. I want to go back and do it again to see what I missed. Maybe I will, but of course, it won't be the same. Life is like that. (Time's Arrow, and so on.)

Anyhow, 8 bouncy, jouncy, roller-coaster morning miles later the Trail spat us out onto Vt Highway 4, and we were back in civilization again. We could hear it for 45 minutes before we arrived. The buzzing undertone of traffic eventually turned into a roar and my dread escalated accordingly. Maybe I'd been in the woods for awhile, but damn, that traffic was moving fast. I leashed up the dogs, ran across the highway and stuck out my thumb.

It was Johnson all over again. Nobody stopped, nobody even slowed down. Trucks, Vans, SUVs, a big wide shoulder to pull over on and plenty of visibility- what more could you want? People just whizzed by. Maybe it was the shepherd, maybe it was my shorts, I don't know. After half a mile I'd had enough. I'd call a taxi. I walked off the highway at the Pico Peak Ski Resort Area. There were some condos and offices and a few construction workers doing a summer remodel. I sat down to rest in the shade near a sign reading Bus Stop, and the girls flopped down nearby. As I was pulling out my glasses and guide book to see if I could find a phone number to call a taxi a little white bus turned off the highway, puttered up the lane, and stopped in front of me. The door of the bus opened and a friendly-looking old driver said "Nice looking dogs you go there."

"Um, thanks. They're amazing dogs. We're doing the Long Trail and they've come all the way from Canada with me." The driver was suitably impressed. "We need a ride to Killington to pick up a box of supplies. I can't walk on the road with them. Traffic is too dangerous."

"Well, I'd let you on but I'm on the way to Rutland right now. I won't be back this way for another hour or so." Then, "are those service dogs? We're only supposed to allow service dogs on the bus." He paused. "It wouldn't matter to me, but every driver is different," he added.

"Well Lyssa had the service dog training," I said indicating my shepherd who was lolling on the grass, "but I never followed through with it."

It was true. A few years back we had gone through the training but I had never taken the last step of asking my doctor for a prescription. I really didn't qualify for needing a service dog. I thought it would be interesting to go through the training with Lyssa and I was very tempted by the idea of having a certificate that would enable me to take her with me everywhere I went. But I knew the whole service dog thing had become a scam for a lot of people, and I wanted no part of lying and abusing the

145

system. Mostly I wanted a well-trained dog who would behave herself in public and would listen to me, and the training certainly accomplished that. (Lyssa was fantastic; I needed the training more than she did.) I also knew the laws. Legally I could tell someone she was a service dog and there was nothing they could do about it. Because of medical privacy laws, no one could ask you what was wrong with you or why you needed a service dog. They could only inquire as to what the dog was trained to do. I'm not sure how you could answer that question without revealing what your medical condition was, but that was how the rules were set up at the time. My thought was that if the dog were unobtrusive and well behaved, no one was likely to challenge you.

Back to the bus driver.

"Look," he said, "it wouldn't matter to me. I like dogs. But the next bus going to Killington, he's a stickler for the rules. Just say they're service dogs, and if he asks you what they do just make something up."

"Um, she helps with mobility." I pointed at Lyssa. "And this one detects seizures," I said, hoisting Tina in my arms. I'm a shitty actor.

"That'll do," he smiled. "Good luck!"

I felt sick about having to tell a bald faced lie. Then I thought about walking with the girls on Highway 4 and decided it was the lesser of two evils. If I had to bend a rule to keep my dogs safe then that rule was made to be bent, I decided. No way was I taking them down 2 miles of road in the blazing sun with non-stop traffic roaring by. The bus to Killington arrived and we went through the charade. The dogs were as good as gold and I was immensely proud of them. There was one other passenger who chattered at me about her poodle, and I listened politely until the sour faced driver dumped us out at the Post Office at 11:45. It was too easy.

The Post Office was closed. An index card taped to the door read "Out to Lunch. Back at 1." I had no choice but to go shopping and the Killington Deli was right next door. Food! It looked pretty casual and safe, so I tied the dogs and our packs to a picnic table outside the front door and dug out my wallet. I don't know what Lyssa would have done if anyone had messed with the packs, but I didn't think anyone would be foolish enough to try. At the deli I bought 2 chicken wraps, a bag of potato chips, some lemonade and a four pound bag of dog food. My plan was to hike straight through the next 7 days, skipping my re-supply in Manchester Center, and finish the trail on time. It was 104.2 miles to the Massachusetts State line. That was 15 miles a day, plus a few miles down the access trail where my brother would meet me. I could do this but I only had 6 days worth of food- 5 in my mail box and 1 left in my pack from having finished the last leg in 5 days instead of 6. I could try stretching the rations to last 7 days, but all three of us were loosing weight. My pants were getting baggy and Lyssa was looking lankier than usual. Tina was the one I worried about the most- she felt light as a feather and I could easily feel her hip bones. You couldn't tell by looking at her, but she was skinny underneath that shaggy coat. Both dogs were eating a premium brand of dog food, formulated for high performance dogs like sled dogs and agility dogs. It had the highest percent of protein and calories per gram of any commercial diet that I could find, and I had tested it out on them for several months before we left. At the rate they were eating they would have been as fat as ticks if we were at home. I supplemented their rations with 100% pure freeze dried turkey, (expensive but very lightweight and nutritious), and tuna-fish from my own lunch rations. It wasn't like they were starving.

Back at the picnic table the dogs and I shared one of the wraps- they got the chicken and a generous portion of dog chow and I got the veggies and chips and lemonade. A few travelers stopped to admire the dogs and take photos of Lyssa looking regal and awesome next to her packs. I charged up my phone on a handy dandy outdoor outlet conveniently located right next to the picnic table, and when it flickered back to life I called home. Hank was in the midst of his morning routine of drinking coffee and feeding the dogs, and he seemed happy to hear from me. I told him my plan for finishing the trail on time- the miles I had yet to cover and my scheme to skip the last mail drop in Manchester Center. "It was really an emergency back-up drop for just in case the trip took longer," I explained. When I mailed the packages I was planning on having a few more days to hike. Later I learned that I really needed to be back to work by October 1, and if I wanted to get home and have a few days of R & R before going back to work I would have to push up my finish date. It was hard to explain. Hank seemed a little skeptical of the whole plan, especially the part where I had to do 15+ miles every day for 7 days in a row. Nothing strengthens my resolve like being told I can't do something! You'd think he would know me better by now. He'd know how much I liked to walk, and how strong and energetic I am. Certainly he should know how driven I can be. Of course he wanted me to win the race and was rooting for me to finish the trail, but he was just being realistic. It was one o'clock, time to go; I gathered dogs and gear and relocated them outside the Post Office.

I was positively euphoric after the good meal and rest. It lasted the whole time I was at the post office and right up to the moment when I hoisted my pack, which was now stuffed with 7 days worth of food on top of everything else. The clerk at the Post Office had looked at me skeptically when I asked for my box, and wanted to see my id. As I fished out my wallet I laughed and said I didn't know if I looked like my photo anymore since I'd been out on the trail for two weeks. "I've seen worse," was all she said. Gotta love these New Englanders!

As I was finishing up stowing my supplies a white pick-up truck pulled up next to the door and a man jumped out. He nodded at me and admired Lyssa. When he came out I asked him if he would mind giving us a lift back to the trail-head and offered to ride in the back of the truck. He was only too happy to oblige, and insisted on having us all ride up front. In the air conditioning, on the leather seats. Then we were back on the trail.

Trail Mantra: "Everyone hikes their own hike."
This is still my hike, but now it is a different hike than it was before. Prior to my decision to set my sights on finishing the Trail on time, the daily challenge had been simple: climb up the Mountains, climb down the Mountains, stay safe. Now the emphasis was shifted: Climb all the mountains between here and the point at least 15 miles from here, and stay safe. Time and mileage took precedence over scenery and enrichment. The last hundred miles of my hike were not as enjoyable or as memorable as the first half. In fact the southern part of the Trail is not as rugged and scenic as the northern part, which is not to say that the south is flat and boring. It is just.....mellower. More open hardwoods, less thick conifers. More swamps. No more of those unique fragile alpine summits with their remnant ice-age flora and fauna; instead there are wooded summits with enormous rickety fire towers which must be climbed in order to appreciate the view. There are more ponds, more lowlands, and a lot more mud! More people too. The reason I chose to hike the "hard way", that is, from North to South, was because I particularly wanted to be sure to have time to experience the "rugged North". I like wild, I like rugged and I prefer less populated trails. If I ran out of time and had to bail out before finishing, I would sacrifice the southern part of the Trail. Now my goal was to finish even if it meant rushing past a few things.

I became a perpetual motion machine- the energizer bunny of late middle aged lady backpackers in Vermont.

About 1/2 of the way up from Highway 4 to Pico Peak I took a little break by a brook to rest and drink some water. As usual I wasn't carrying any water. With 7 days worth of food the pack was heavier than ever, and I felt every ounce. I might have to load up on water if I couldn't make it to a good camping place with a water source- I dreaded the thought of adding another 4 pounds to my load. The map showed nothing- no creeks or ponds or anything until well beyond the summit of Killington. I was digging around in my pack deep beneath my massive bag of provisions to locate my guidebook and see if it had any more information when a hiker approached- a familiar figure I had last seen at Taft Lodge in the early morning fog on Mount Mansfield. He had been Northbound, and his trail name was Rockfish. He was the nerdy guy with the giant pack had slept in the bunk above me and had shown me a video he'd made of the infamous ladder gap. I had thought of him the day we made it around the ladder, wishing I could tell him the story of how we found the way. But he had been heading North; I would never see him again, and yet here he was, coming up the trail behind me! "Rockfish! You're going the wrong way," I shouted. Rockfish has giant legs that match his giant pack. "I finished the trail," he said. "Now I'm just out for a hike before I have to catch the train back to Detroit." Whoa, that sounded crazy! Crazy, nerdy Rockfish who had left the door to the lodge unlatched and let the door bang on its hinges half the night- I was astounded at how wonderful it was to see him again and share my story of climbing up ladder gap, and all of the other adventures I'd had since that foggy morning at Taft. I listened to his stories too, remembering those rugged highlights of the north- Whiteface, Madonna, Belvedere, Tillotson, Hay-stack, and Jay. I asked him a million questions and listened with genuine interest to everything- his story about his Italian Grandmother who really knew how to cook, his love for the Beatles, his delight at the second hand junk stores in Schenectady. How surprised and happy his mother would be when he got off the train in Detroit. We chatted enthusiastically about gear and other trails we had done. Rockfish had completed the Appalachian Trail and had done the PCT, twice. He was the real deal.

Rockfish solved my water problem by suggesting that I

spend the night at Pico Camp, which was 0.4 miles down the old Sherburne Pass Trail off of the Long Trail, but almost certainly had water. If it turned out to be dry he would give me all of his large supply since he was heading back down the Sherburne Pass Trail to Highway 4 to catch the bus to Rutland. The next few miles flew by and I completely forgot to notice how heavy my pack felt. At Pico Peak Shelter we stopped for the night and Rockfish made notes on my map about all the watering holes and highlights of the trail ahead, and then he was gone, bound for Detroit.

I'm not what you'd call a real social person. I prefer to keep a low profile when it comes to interactions with other people. I understand dogs better than humans. But out on the trail something weird happens- I'm actually happy to see people, and happy to stop and visit with them. Lyssa and Tina like people more than I do, and so I let them be my ambassadors, my meeters & greeters. Most hikers have passed the dog test and are already friends with my girls by the time I enter the picture. So out on the trail I have a lot of friends. There is something magical about Trail Friends. It's hard to explain. Hiking the same trail binds you together somehow, into a community. Trail friends can be the most unlikely individuals you'd ever expect to connect with, thrown together by chance, but they become special people who you will never forget and always hold dear. It's Trail Magic- another gift of the Long Trail.

Pico camp was blessed with a tiny spring of clean clear water coming out of the rock, and a perfect flat tent site near by, so the girls and I were very happy to claim it and not have to share the cabin with several burly male occupants. We split the second chicken wrap and hit the sack at sundown. I did the numbers. We'd come 11 trail miles, not bad. Tomorrow morning we'd tackle Killington Peak, and then it was all downhill, more or less, all the way to Clarendon Gorge. Rockfish loved Clarendon Gorge. You weren't supposed to spend the night near the

Gorge anymore, but Rockfish said there was a large area where people still camped. Discreetly. It was a great place to swim and spend the day exploring, he said. I'd have to go a little further in order to make my 15 mile minimum however. I set my sights on the Minerva Hinchey shelter. Rockfish's notes said there was an okay source of water there. Dear old Rockfish.

We were in the home stretch- seven marathon days of non-stop pushing for miles. Everything in me was on a mission to finish- I didn't have time or energy to think about anything except time and mileage, mileage and time. I had left the old obsessions behind, somewhere north of Dave's Peak, or maybe Mt Horrid. There was a thought. What if everyone left their troubles there- that would explain why it was so Horrid. Ha.

The next thing I knew it was 5 am and my alarm was ringing. It was time to go.

Chapter 8

September 17, 2016

Day 15
Clarendon Gorge

The dogs and I departed Pico Camp as early as we could, just as it was getting light enough to see the trail. One of the men from the shelter stopped on his way to the outhouse to wave us off. "Have a good hike!" "You too, have a good hike!" As we tromped up the trail I heard the faint bang of the cabin door slamming. It felt good to be moving.

Freedom! For the next 3 miles we had the early morning high elevation forest all to ourselves. It was silent and still in the dim light of dawn. The air was crisp and rarefied, rich with damp, earthy odor. I was startled when an early morning hiker passed by us, heading north. He gave us a slight nod and continued on without speaking or slowing down. Later I read his entry in the log book at Cooper Lodge- he'd spent an unhappy, restless night alone at the lodge, haunted and frightened by every squeak and scurry of the many mice and chipmunks residing there.

Cooper Lodge, near the summit of Killington Mountain, was creepy, to be sure. On the damp dirt floor I found a bag of trash from a fast food restaurant, bits of which had been scattered all over by the resident rodents. Lyssa kept the mice at bay while I gathered up the trash, and we passed it off to a northbound hiker with an empty pack who was headed down to Killington village for a few days of R & R. Then we started downhill.

We hadn't been hiking for long when we met another northbound hiker laboring up the steep ascent to the summit. She was wearing a Mad River Glen T-shirt and I couldn't help but stop and visit with her. Did she know my brother Dale? She sure did. Not only knew him, but skied with him and his wife Wendy, and were great friends. Her name was Maggie. Later Dale told me funny stories about Maggie involving someone falling off the chairlift. Meeting someone on the trail who not only knew my brother but had spent time with him and was actually quite fond of him kind of blew me away. I knew the younger Dale, the little kid-Dale with whom I'd grown up; she knew the current-Dale, the middle-aged adult Dale, the ski-patroller and all-around good guy to be friends with, and he was still the same guy. I was full of warm fuzzies all the way down to Clement Shelter. Vermont. My brother's family was here. I was beginning to think that maybe I belonged here too.

Governor Clement Shelter is an historic old building, and a classic Vermont Trail Shelter. It also is situated near a wonderful broad shallow brook, which was running full with clean clear cold water. I spent an hour washing myself, changing clothes and scrubbing all of my dirty socks and skivvies. The girls snoozed in the sun on the banks of the brook while I rearranged my pack, hanging all of my wet laundry on the outside to dry. Refreshed, we took off for the next leg- a long low elevation cross-country ramble through forests, fields and farmlands, crossing several dirt back-roads and more brooks, until we reached Clarendon Shelter, and then finally the highway crossing with the trail-head for Clarendon Gorge.

The path down to the bridge was packed with a continuous stream of day hikers and picnickers in flip-flops, tennis shoes and spandex, carting ice chests, strollers, fat

MP 179.1 Governor Clement Shelter

Upper Cold River Rd

Gilman Rd

Cold River Rd

Keifer Rd

103

Clarendon Lookout

Beacon Hill

Lottery Rd

Clarendon Shelter   MP 184.9

Clarendon Gorge

103

Minerva Hinchey Shelter

Camp Sept 17

Patch Hollow

Bear Mtn 2262

140

MP 192.2

Sugar Hill Rd

Cairns   Greenwall Shelter

Map 11: Clarendon Gorge and Minerva Hinchey Shelter

155

adorable little chihuahuas and toddlers. They stared at me with my giant backpack waving it's pennants of wool socks and underwear. I smiled benignly and focused on keeping Lyssa and Tina from scaring the shit out of them. My girls were delighted to be seeing so many potential friends reeking of yummy picnic smells. At the bridge I stopped long enough to ask someone to take our picture for us, and then wasted no time heading for higher ground. Up.

A thousand feet of uphill in 2 and a half miles shouldn't have been so hard, but by Airport Lookout my quadriceps were screaming in protest. I stopped to call and check in with Hank, and massaged my legs. Lyssa was still on a leash. Every time I let her off she worked herself into a frenzy of chipmunk hunting- dashing off and pouncing every five minutes. I couldn't believe she still had so much strength and energy while I felt exhaustion at every upwards step. At the rate I was moving it was questionable whether we'd make it to Minerva Hinchey before dark.

Well, we made it, but the only because of Lyssa. 45 minutes beyond the gorge my arms were exhausted from holding onto her leash, and so I fashioned sort of a harness around my waist and butt and attached her to it and used my weight to apply the brakes. It worked. Not only that, but by watching the trail and talking to her I could actually take advantage of her pulling on me to help give me a lift on the steep parts. I'm not ashamed to say I let that dog pull me up the ridge like a draft horse. It was a little tricky steering whenever a nearby chipmunk sounded an alarm, but I learned to anticipate her sudden leaps and parley them into added impetus. We strode into the shelter camp like champions, with plenty of light to do chores and set up camp. Lyssa flopped down near the tent and didn't move the rest of the night, except to sit up when I brought her dinner with extra rations of tuna on top. My big beautiful strong faithful shepherd. She was my best friend, my partner, my soul-mate. She was all I needed in this life.

A backpacking trip is an escape into a whole different world; it's total immersion in alternate reality. Life is pared down to simple basics- eat, drink, sleep, walk. Repeat. Walking is what you do, and everything else is built around accomplishing the simple task of putting one foot in front of the other. All other obligations and requirements are gone. When your are in motion on the trail

And Tina. I needed her too. We all needed each other.

your mind is freed to wander down trails of its own. The steady rhythm of the pace generates a Zen which enables focus; the mind travels deeply into old haunts and discovers new places to explore- new ideas, new insights, new paradigms. I don't know where I heard it, but it's true: free your feet and your mind will follow.

Lyssa was a fantastic companion and a perfect partner for me on the trail. But we wouldn't/couldn't be on the trail forever. Our trip was a hard-earned vacation from real life, a life to which I clearly did not want to return under the same terms and conditions as had existed previously. I wanted a change. I had a rough outline of what I wanted-

less stress, less responsibility, less work and more time to see the world- but much beyond that I was fuzzy on the details. The long days of hiking would be the perfect time to think about those details. I had 6 days left to figure out the rest of my life. And it was time to deal with the elephant in the room. Hello, Elephant.

When I married Hank he seemed perfect, and probably he was. He liked dogs, music, hiking and ice cream. He was easy on the ear and on the eye. He was a dreamer with a gentle soul. Together we dreamed big dreams, like climbing the highest peak in every state. We moved to the Sierras and bought a house and collected a few more mutts to replace my old Phoebe, whose biological clock had been set for 15 years exactly and not a day longer. I did most of the bread-winning since I had no trouble finding good paying work, and Hank, not so much. But it was okay because I had a house in the woods, a pack of beautiful dogs, and a gentle musical partner. I grabbed hold with both hands and jumped right on that treadmill. We lived happily ever after, for awhile.

A few years went by and the fabric of our lives began to wear thin and fray at the edges. Hank battled with clin-ical depression and I struggled to give him whatever he needed to find happiness. Stuff: a computer, hardwood flooring, a truck, and lots of music. The house always needed something- a roof, a new deck, finishing the basement, a new pump and a septic tank. I took on more and more work shifts, sometimes working around the clock when I filled in at the emergency clinic. We had to have more money, Hank said. He tried his hand at a few things but it was mostly on me. I started to feel like a rat trapped in an endless spinning treadmill, never getting ahead. Exhausting myself. I burned out on the veterinary profession and began to wonder whether my partner was a lazy self-centered free-loader instead of the easy going gentle loving person I had married. Seeing no way out, I starting succumbing to depression also. I lost my sense of humor. We fought a lot. I was too committed to quit but

I was desperate for a change. Eventually my body broke instead.

In 2000 I injured my shoulder while trying to lift a boulder for a retaining wall on the side of our house. Stubbornly I ignored the injury and kept working. Within 3 months I was not able to lift my left arm at all. The ligaments holding my arm in place were torn, and my body was trying to heal the instability by freezing the shoulder into solid immobility with inflammatory adhesions. I couldn't move my fingers without shooting pains in my shoulder. I had no choice but to stop working and go on disability. Despite the pain and the loss of use of my arm, it was a great relief to stop working and have time for myself. It was like my body had bought my freedom from enslavement in the materialistic rat race by sacrificing a limb- I had given an arm to save my life. I started the new millennium with 2 surgeries and months of physical therapy. As I began to heal my natural restlessness and energy began to return, and I started walking with the dogs. At first I went down in the canyon behind our house which borders on the Eldorado National Forest. I found old logging trails, mining camps and sluice-ways from gold mining days. Then as summer progressed I began to explore the higher elevations and discovered Desolation Wilderness, Carson Pass, and a wealth of alpine trail networks within an hour's drive, practically in my backyard. All of my childhood dreams and ambitions of long distance hiking and traveling started to return. By the end of the summer I was able to return to work, but I was determined to find a way to balance my work and my health and fitness- to take every opportunity to get outside and go up to the mountains.

For many years Hank was a willing and able companion for going hiking in the mountains. I pushed for more ambitious hikes, overnights and multi-day backpacking trips. In 2008 I turned 50 and I proposed that we do something epic and unforgettable. Together we dreamed up the idea of doing the John Muir Trail. I seized the idea with a passion and after awhile Hank signed on as well. The initial hesitation was because he was turning 70, and while he wasn't in bad shape, he'd need to do some work to tackle a 3 week 215 mile trek in the sierra high country. The trip was epic and unforgettable. I enjoyed every minute and every step; Hank hung in there and made it to the end with me. We kept a journal and I took a thousand photos. Afterwards I re-lived the trip over and over, going through the photos and remembering each day's adventures. For me it was the beginning of the realization of my dreams; for Hank it was sort of one last hurrah. His enthusiasm for the rigors of the trail waned, as he fell prey to aches and pains of advancing years. When his son died suddenly of a heart attack, (Bret was my age, almost exactly), Hank's battles with depression worsened. He continued casual forays to go rock climbing with a few older retired acquaintances, but slowly he began to spend more time snoozing in the lazy boy and the distance which he could walk or hike became less and less. No longer could he handle the 10 or 12 mile days, even in a light pack. Now he's good for a mile or two before the hips and knees start aching. I can't fault him for having to slow down. We're all heading that direction whether we like it or not. But I'm not ready to slow down yet and I sure don't intend to do so a minute before I have to. So eventually, painfully, I started going without him, with other friends or finally just with my dogs. To my surprise I found out that I was perfectly fine going on mountain adventures by myself. Well, not really by myself because I always had my dogs along. They were not just casual companions, they were delightful and devoted friends, bringing immeasurable joy and pleasure to every expedition. In 2011 I started on a project to do the Tahoe Rim Trail in a series of weekend hikes. Hank would drop me off at a trail head and pick me up a day or two later at the other end of the section. The first year I did the east side of Lake Tahoe with Jeremiah, Tina, Lucy and sometimes Partner. Then came Lyssa, who appeared to be born for the trail and destined to be my constant companion. Our first trip together was a four day trip to the Ventana Wilderness at Big Sur, and it was as if she had discovered her purpose in life. She took to the trail like a fish to water. I've never hiked alone since I found Lyssa.

The John Muir Trail gave me my first taste of long distance hiking. Like an appetizer, it was a taste that only gave me a craving for more. On crazy busy demanding days at work, juggling a thousand demands on my time and attention, I'd ruefully remember life on the trail where my only task was to put one foot in front of the other, climb up the mountain, climb down the mountain, eat, drink plenty of water, don't loose any gear and don't get hurt. Or lost. Simple, straight forward, physically demanding for sure, but vastly preferable to the stress and chaos of civilization.

So when I went off to the mountains Hank stayed at home and took care of the older non-hiker dogs, and watered the plants. He dropped me off at the beginning of a trail-head and picked me up at the other end. He liked being an armchair hiker, and I couldn't have done it without his support. Sometimes he met us along the way at a road crossing with an ice chest full of fresh fruit and goodies and fresh rations for the dogs. Sometimes we'd swap dogs- trading tired out sore-footed ones for rested up ones. He took good care of them. I'd send him gps coordinates and photos along the way and he'd follow my progress on his computer. He spent a lot of time on the computer in those days. Sometimes he'd stare at the screen for hours on end, barely even acknowledging my comings and goings. I felt invisible. Many times I thought it likely that he never missed me when I was gone, so little did he seem to notice me. The exception was when he got hungry and had to make his own dinner, but I always left plenty of frozen pizza. That's all he needed.

Leaving Hank was never really an option. I can't say that I hadn't thought about it a few times in the past when things had gotten rough- times when maybe the only reason we stayed together was because of the dogs, or

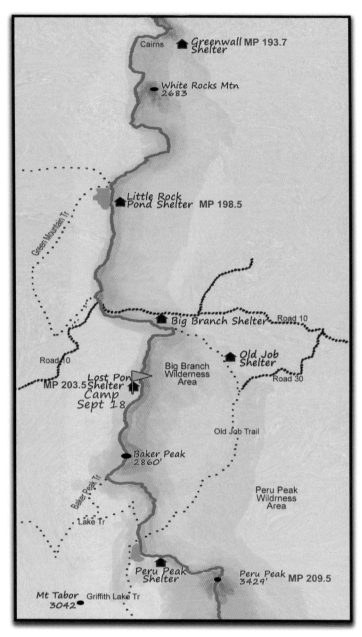

Cairns
Greenwall MP 193.7 Shelter

White Rocks Mtn 2683

Little Rock Pond Shelter MP 198.5

Green Mountain Tr

Big Branch Shelter   Road 10

Old Job Shelter

Road 10

MP 203.5 Lost Pond Shelter Camp Sept 18

Big Branch Wilderness Area

Road 30

Old Job Trail

Baker Peak 2860'

Baker Peak Tr

Peru Peak Wildrness Area

Lake Tr

Peru Peak Shelter

Peru Peak 3429'   MP 209.5

Mt Tabor 3042   Griffith Lake Tr

Map 12 White Rocks, Lost Pond Shelter and Peru Peak

162

maybe because neither of us had the energy or impetus to file for divorce. But when I went to Vermont it was different. I had never gone this far away from home for this long. Vermont was on the other side of the country and might as well have been on the other side of the planet. This time I had stretched the bond out to a thin, tenuous thread. It had never been so close to breaking, but I had no intention or thought of breaking it. I was just running away for awhile, having an adventure, taking a break, and recharging my spirit. I would come home, and for now home was still in California, with Hank and the rest of the dogs. For now.

September 18, 2016

Day 16
White Rock Cairns

5 more days to go. The girls hardly moved all night long, but seem peppy and ready to roll when we hit the trail again just as it is getting light. The day seems to be having trouble making up it's mind whether to be a rainy day or just settle for damp and cloudy. By the time we cross Highway 140 it's leaning towards damp and cloudy, which suits me fine, because soon we are climbing up into the cloud forest again. What better weather could there be for visiting the cairn gardens? These whimsical creations are a treat to discover and admire, and take me totally by surprise. I took some photos, but the camera failed to capture the aura of magic and wonder cloaking this unexpected display of sculpture. I love that human hands have shaped these raw materials from nature into something still totally natural and also totally delightful.

I was amazed at my dogs when we hit the trail the next morning. You know how dogs get all excited when they see you put on your walking shoes and they know they are going out for a walk? And you have to spell the word W-A-L-K out loud instead of saying it because you don't

163

want them to know what you have in mind and get all excited and bounce around like maniacs before you can get them on the leash and out the door? That was Tina and Lyssa. As soon as I hefted my pack they were bouncing down the trail ahead of me, as if going for a walk was the most exciting thing they could imagine doing today. Not a hint of being tired or sore or reluctant to trot off down the never-ending trail and start the day. Their pep and cheerfulness was infectious and inspired me as I traipsed along behind them.

The misty morning weather made it hard to know how to dress for the day. I didn't want to get wet if the mist thickened or morphed into actual rain, but I didn't want to get hot either, so I settled for rain pants over shorts. By the time I was halfway up Bear Mountain I'd warmed up enough so that I didn't mind getting a little wet, and the rain pants went back into the pack. We were shrouded in a cocoon of mist as we walked. A few other hikers passed by, shrouded in their own silent cocoons, offering only the slightest nod or wave of acknowledgment. Spooky.

Crossing highway 140, we entered the White Rocks Recreation Area and started climbing. Everything was green and shrouded in gray mists. I loved the feeling of being in a cloud forest. A dream forest in the clouds. It was like the legendary magical mists of Avalon, hidden from the eyes of the real world, lost in another era all its own, where time passes more slowly and the laws of nature don't work exactly the same as they do in the real world. Strange magical unexpected things happen. The cairn gardens, so surreal and beautiful in the mists, proved the magical quality of the day. I was totally enthralled by the cairn gardens and tried to capture their magic on my camera, but only obtained images of stacks of rocks in fog. You had to be there to feel the magic of them I guess. I wanted to share my delight at seeing these beautiful whimsical creations with someone who would understand my excitement and appreciation- there was

The White Rock Cairns

only one person who would fit the bill and that was Hank. I knew he would like to hear about my discovery and how magical it felt. So I called him and told him all about it and sent him photos of Tina and Lyssa amongst the cairns. He understands stuff like that, which is why I am going back home to California when I am done. He knows me.

We wandered along up through the cloud forest for a long time. Once a heavy-set northbound hiker came huffing and puffing up the trail ahead of us. He was carrying an awful lot of weight, much of it not in his pack, and was bundled up in rain gear. The way he appeared to be sweating I figured he was wetter inside the rain gear than out. "Where are the white rocks," he demanded, "this is supposed to be the white rocks recreation area." "Nothin' here but these green ones," I said. He laughed and huffed and puffed on up the trail. Everyone hikes their own hike, I thought. I was glad to be hiking mine.

Eventually we arrived at Little Rock Pond and left behind the forest in the clouds. The next 2.2 miles along Little Black Branch creek would have been a long muddy slog except for the grace of the Green Mountain Club workers who have laid an impressive pathway of stepping stones, (boulders really), almost the whole distance. Negotiating the boulders took some exhausting focus and concentration, but eventually we arrived at the parking lot, crossed the road and dove into the forest again on the way to Big Branch Shelter. It was mid-afternoon and we were well on target to make it to Lost Pond Shelter. Less than 2 miles left to chalk up a respectable 15 mile day.

On the way up to Lost Pond Shelter I actually got angry with Lyssa, probably for about the first time, ever. It was a measure of how hard I was pushing myself and how focused I was on time and miles. I'm also pretty sure it had something to do with a moose.

If I could change anything about my dog, it would be to lower the gain on her predatory instincts. Lyssa is the best dog ever at staying with me on the trail and coming when I call her, but all it takes is one squeak from a mouse or a marmot and her brains fly out her ears. She pounces before another thought can enter the space that a moment ago was occupied by a brain, but now contains only one thing, which is pouncing on squeaky thing. Lyssa has pounced on several thousand squeaky things in the bush on our travels, but to my knowledge she has actually ever caught but one or two. She's strictly into catch and release. Well, she would release them if she ever caught them. The one time she caught a baby marmot I made her release it and it waddled into the bush unharmed. So she's a pouncer but not a killer. I didn't know what she would do if we encountered larger animals, however. A couple of times in the Sierras we crossed paths with cattle, (they still have summer grazing permits in some Wilderness Areas!) and Lyssa quickly learned to leave them alone. Besides, they don't squeak. On occasion she has chased deer, disappearing into the bush long enough make me more than a little anxious about whether she would find her way back. Invariably she would reappear trotting towards me along

*the trail from ahead, panting like a freight train. I usual-
ly put her on leash if there are deer in the neighborhood.
Leashing her up stops the risk of her getting lost, injured or
getting her saddle bags ripped off on a snag, but it creates
another problem- I have to hang onto her! Most of the time
things go well and she takes it easy. But just as I am getting
lulled into thinking how considerate and well behaved she
is--Squeak!-- brains fly out the ears and pounce happens.
If I have enough warning I can usually brace myself for
impact, but once in awhile I get jerked off my feet, which
is very annoying, especially in the afternoon when we are
negotiating some endless rocky downhill climb. At the
lower elevations the Vermont mountains the forests are full
of chipmunks: evil creatures who know how to torture an
overgrown coyote on a leash attached to a tired human.
They see us coming. So there I was, grinding up the last hill
of the day to Lost Pond Shelter- counting pole plants and
thinking about nothing. Lyssa was unleashed when something squeaked and off she went. But instead of playing the
usual game of hide and seek at the base of the tree, my dog
kept charging into the brush and was soon out of earshot. 5
or 10 minutes later I'm fuming up the trail bellowing at the
top of my lungs so that when she gives up on the chase she
will hear me and know where to find me. I'm angry with
her for causing me all this anxiety. Plus it is just embar-
rassing, because other hikers hear me yelling and think I
need help. When she finally does reappear, I snap the leash
on her and cuss at her. Her bear bell is missing but at least
the saddle-bags are unscathed. I hate it that she ran off
like that and I hate it that I feel so angry with her. She's my
best friend. She's traveled this whole way with me, through
thick and thin- mountains and cliffs and mud pits- and never ever complained about anything. Not even when I made
her ride in the car for four days straight or when loaded
her with 7 days worth of dog food. I've never yelled at her,
ever, or hardly even ever raised my voice at her. But I'm
tired, dirty, hungry, and I smell so bad I can hardly stand*

myself. I can't stop to take a shower or wash my clothes, or have a decent meal. And this stupid Trail is still going up. Always up. Damn dog!

I keep her tied to me the rest of the day, keep her tied up while I set up camp and make dinner, and I make her sleep inside the tent with me. During the night it starts raining, and I wake up to find a giant wall of warm dry fur beside me. On the other side, Tina is curled up in a warm silky ball tucked under the flap of my sleeping bag. I am so glad they are there so close to me. I love them beyond measure. How on earth could I have been angry? It's all wrong- I've pushed too hard and lost sight of priorities. And now it's raining, heavy hard steady rain. Suddenly I know that making it to the Southern terminus is not more important than taking care of my best friends, and it is not worth the cost of compromising my relationship with them. These dogs trust me without question or hesitation and they would follow me anywhere. Their welfare is 100% my responsibility. If Lyssa gets lost or injured it's my fault for putting her in jeopardy.

I am fortunate to own this sweet mellow dog who is almost always obedient eager to please me. She hardly needed any training- she made it too easy for me. I was a lax, lazy and indulgent trainer. I didn't have the discipline or take the time to deal with little issues like pulling or ignoring squeaky varmints when she was on leash. And now I expected perfection from her without having taught her the rules.

In the still, dark, small hours of the morning, when my mind is fresh and free of the rubble of the day, clarity comes. The following truths are clear: #1 I see that my preoccupation with the goal of reaching the "finish line" is damaging my relationship with Lyssa and Tina who are my most important responsibility to care for. The Southern Terminus means nothing to them- just another post to sniff, perhaps. It's my goal, not theirs. They are happy simply to be with me. It is not fair for me to force this goal on them if it is causing problems. OK. #2- the chipmunk issue. I have a nearly perfect dog who has this minor flaw which is that she can't resist pouncing on things that squeak and scurry in the brush. I need to communicate to her that sometimes this is OK and sometimes it is not OK. I need to teach her the difference between being on and off leash, and that leash time is not hunting time. Period. She is smart enough to learn this if I am smart enough to teach her. I have the skills and expertise to teach her because I have been well trained myself. It's work- focusing, paying attention, anticipating, responding and rewarding. Communicating with my dog loud and clear. Teaching a 90 pound shepherd with a strong prey drive and no discipline- I have my work cut out for me! But it is a good thing to do and it will pay off for both of us, improve our relationship and make for a more enjoyable and safer hike for both of us. That stuff is more important than the finish line. #3 It's raining. If it rains like this all day, and it might, we will all get wet. I have decent rain gear but it will not keep me dry in hours of steady downpour. Being out in such conditions would not be enjoyable and might even be dangerous if we get hypothermic. Solution- If necessary we will stop and hole up in a shelter somewhere. There are a few possibilities along the way, including Bromley Mountain. If this happens it will mean that we will not finish the Trail, and that's okay. We will have given it an honest effort. No regrets, no shame. No sooner does this last insight trickle up through the mental murk and into the realm of certainty than I immediately start feeling lighter and happier. When we crawl out of the tent the day is breaking and the rain has stopped.

Lyssa is about as perfect as a dog can be,
but I need a little work.

Chapter 9

September 19, 2016

Day 17
Bromley

It stopped raining but the tent fly and insert were dripping wet and covered with pine needles and debris from the forest floor that had kicked up during the downpour. I lugged everything down to the unoccupied lean-to and draped the tent on pegs under the overhang so that it could start to drip dry while I fed the dogs and sipped my coffee. I was in no hurry to stuff the wet dirty fabric into my pack. I wasn't in a hurry for anything. In the damp morning air the tent was not in a hurry to dry out either. When my coffee was gone I attacked the tent with my all-purpose bandanna, brushing it as clean as I could before rolling it up. Wet fabric is heavier than dry, even when it is "hyperlight," but I wasn't complaining. Everything else was dry; it was a small price to pay.

Despite the rainstorm and my having attained enlightenment at least as far as dog and mileage priorities were concerned, we were on the trail by 7 am as usual. The morning started with an easy gradual climb up a nondescript summit called Baker Peak. It was the same angle of ascent as yesterday's climb up to Lost Pond Shelter, but seemed much easier in the fresh early morning. I focused on walking in the moment, counting my pole plants, and lost myself in thought. I had a lot to think about. In walking the trail I had jettisoned the weight of the obsessions of the past 5 years of caring for my parents and others to whom I felt obligation. I had come to terms with my own mortality and reclaimed permission to take care of my own needs and desires, permission to try to fulfill dreams long postponed or set aside for the sake of others. I had earned the right to be a little bit selfish. I had found reserves of strength and wisdom, and the self-confidence to know that I could handle big challenges. I now knew I had the strength and resourcefulness to take control of my own life and change it in the direction I wanted to go. The basic vision was clear: work less, travel more, stay active. I just needed to figure out the details and get my financial ducks in a row. It was do-able, just like Mount Mansfield and the rest of those crazy steep summits. I could do it. But the devil was in the details, and the first question was Where. California? Or elsewhere?

In July when I came out to visit Dale and scout out the Trail I started to fall in love with Vermont. In retrospect maybe it was more like an old flame being rekindled. Vermont was green and wet. The lush rolling countryside was eye candy for me. With the drought in California it had been ages since I had seen such vast expanses of emerald green. Everything seemed so clean and tidy. Buildings were freshly painted and well maintained. My brother explained that one reason Vermont seemed so unspoiled compared to neighboring states was because there were no billboards in Vermont. He was right. A state that cared enough about environmental aesthetics that it had outlawed billboards- wow!- that was my kind of state!

I took photos of the green fields, pastures and hillsides under crisp blue July skies with puffy white clouds and showed them to my friends in California. They couldn't believe it was real. It looked like a Hollywood set in a feel-good Hallmark movie, or a tourist advertisement for Ireland or Wales. "I could live here," I thought. Dale asked me: "what would you do in the wintertime?" I didn't know. Go see my friends in California I suppose. Or stay inside and write books. All I would need was a good wood-stove, good insulation and good wifi and I'd be happy. We'd be happy. (I had to include Hank in my scheme.) Oh, and privacy and good fences for the dogs. And a good view of the mountains. That's all I needed. Dale had long entertained dreams of retiring from his job in New Jersey,

selling the house and moving to Vermont. He was through with the overcrowding and congestion of central Jersey. He could go anytime, he said. The thought of living close to my family felt great. I did a quick check on the Real Estate market in Vermont and decided that houses were generally more affordable than in California. By the time the weekend was over I'd mentally laid half the groundwork for moving my self and my family 3,500 mile across the country. But first I'd come back in September and walk the whole state from Canada to the Massachusetts border, and when I reached the end of the trail I would know the answer. So here I was with 4 days to go and I still didn't have a plan.

The sky seemed to fluctuate between indefinite shades of gray and white; my clothing and skin were damp and

Mt Tabor
3043'

Styles Peak MP 211.2
3394'

Peru Peak
Wilderness Area

Big Branch
Wilderness
Area

Mad Tom Notch Rd

MP 214.8

Bromley Mtn
3260'

Bromley
Shelter

Bromley
Ski
Area

7

30

30

Spruce Peak
2040'

Camp
Sept 19

Spruce Peak MP 221.1
Shelter

Prospect Rock

William B
Douglas
Shelter

Map 13: Peru Peak, Bromley, and Spruce Peak

174

grubby feeling even though it had not rained again since the very early cloudburst. The trail seemed to wander aimlessly through the forest until it finally dumped us out at Griffith Lake, a lovely spot with a long puncheon paved tunnel of trees all along the eastern shore. A passing hiker earlier in the trip had told me it was a great place to stop for a swim, but the idea of getting wetter was not particularly appealing. It would surely be impossible to dry off after swimming, I thought. The girls and I kept walking, happy to be moving. It felt good to be walking, and so we did. We didn't even slow down, really, until Bromley. I'd heard that there was a really nice lodge with a good view on Bromley and I was looking forward to checking it out. If the weather happened to turn foul it would be a good place to hang out for awhile. In the back of my mind I was also thinking that there might be day hikers up there who might just happen to have brought too much lunch with them, and maybe I could score a peanut butter sandwich. Don't ask me why this thought was sitting there in my brain, it just materialized and sat there waiting for me to notice it.

Bromley was not the highest peak of the day, but it has this really sneaky false summit on the north side, followed by a little dip, and then a super butt-kicker steep ascent up to the real summit. Usually Bromley Mountain is a popular spot for day hikers and peak baggers- it has a nice open summit with a view, a good shelter, and some cool rocks to play on. I expected to find the usual small crowd as I popped over the ridge to the summit, grunting and cussing at the last unexpected bit of steep climb. But there was only one other person, a day hiker, trying to sunbathe on the summit rock. Cloudbathing was more like it. Whatever, Lyssa put an end to it in short order. She is an expert face licker, and evidently this gentleman tasted delicious. That is how I met my very own Trail Angel.

I didn't like him at first. With a shaved head and thick New Jersey accent, I thought he was kind of a hot shot.

175

But he got all of my attention when he said "you look like you could use some food. I have an extra sandwich- do you want it?" I sat up. "What kind?" It wasn't that I was hungry; I was completely empty. "Fried egg. With cheese. On a roll." He tossed me a foil package. As I gobbled down the sandwich in sort of one long continuous bite I mumbled that this was the best food I had ever eaten in my entire life, and it was true. It was a magical sandwich. I'm pretty sure that I would not have been able to finish the Trail without it. A simple egg and cheese sandwich could not have been so delicious, so nourishing and so strengthening. It filled more than my belly- it filled me up with happiness all the way to my toes. I fairly flew the rest of the way to Spruce Ledge Shelter, 17.5 miles, my best day yet!

I didn't even get his name. He was the first trail angel I ever met and I wasn't sure if it was good etiquette to ask for names, or if they preferred to be anonymous. I did learn that he was from New Jersey and liked to come up here to the mountains to get rid of the stress of his normal life. He hadn't done the whole trail, but had done day hikes over most of it. And he always brought an extra sandwich in case he met a hungry backpacker like me. He believed in paying it forward, he said. We talked for quite awhile, but I don't remember much of the conversation. I mentioned my husband Hank, and he mentioned his wife, and that was that. We looked at the map and he said he reckoned I would make it to Stratton Mountain about this time tomorrow and he'd been thinking he might go up that way tomorrow also and would I like another egg sandwich? I felt a little guilty, like I was cheating somehow. Accepting favors from a strange man. But I said yes. If you read the book "Wild" or watched the movie you know there was an awful lot of sex and drugs in that story. I'm not anything like Cheryl Strayed, and egg sandwiches were as wild as I got. My Angel made it clear that he did not want anything in return. It was a no-strings-attached egg sandwich. "Just pay it forward," was all he said.

As I flew down the trail I called Hank and told him about the miraculous egg sandwich. Then I called Dale and told him I thought I was actually going to make it to the end of the trail on time, and he should plan on meeting me there unless something unforeseen came up. I knew I could make it because I had an egg sandwich in my belly. Not only that, but I had the promise of another egg sandwich tomorrow. It was almost like..... a lunch date! With a complete stranger. A secret tryst on a mountain-top in Vermont. Later I showed a photo of my Angel to a friend back home and she said "Wow, he's hot," like maybe there was potentially something more to be had than a magical sandwich. Like, maybe it was not simply a case of a philanthropically inclined day hiker giving sustenance to an obviously starving through hiker. I'll confess that I don't have the best marriage in the world, but I've never felt tempted to stray beyond the bounds of it. Maybe I'm just a goody-goody type of person, or maybe it's because I have my feelings and passions so locked away that I don't even remember how to engage in them anymore. For awhile now I've suspected it's the latter. I love my dogs without reservation or boundaries, but people are kept at arm's length. The only time a dog ever broke my heart was when it reached the end of it's life and passed away, but people were not so trustworthy.

I'm still trying to figure out the Love thing. I've been around it for 58 years but I can't come up with a satisfactory definition. Recently I thought I'd figured out a solid piece of it, to wit: Love is a willingness to put up with a lot of shit (even to the apparent detriment of one's own well-being) in order to attain or preserve the opportunity to be close to someone, whether emotionally, sexually, or simply in physical proximity as in sharing the same space or resources. That's kind of where I'm at with it right now.

The other day I noticed a piece of artwork I'd left hanging on the wall in the bedroom after we had reclaimed it from occupation by Mom. It reads "Love is Patient, Love is Kind, Love Never Fails". I kept it because I knew I would always need the reminder to be patient, kind and steadfast. Actually, I had originally justified saving the piece by suggesting that it might be helpful to my husband, who would, on occasion, loose his temper. Unexpectedly and irrationally, in my opinion. He could lash out with a lightening fast and unbelievably vicious jab that would leave me gasping and reeling for breath, not knowing what hit me. Maybe he would see the poster and remember to take a deep breath before he reacted in rage. It seemed like a good idea, but I knew that it wouldn't help. He flew off the handle way to fast to have time to take in the words, even writ large and hanging in front of his nose. The only thing that made a difference was whether I had the grace and presence of mind to avoid pushing his anger buttons. I have a knack for pushing buttons.

I looked at the sign again, studying the words, analyzing and parsing the meaning. The intent. Two adjectives, one verb, all modifying a four letter word that can be used as a verb or a noun. In this case probably a noun. A noun, meaning....what? Something intangible, certainly. I could think of lots of words describing love but I couldn't come up with a solid definition of what it is. It's a feeling. That was a start. Love is a feeling, that when felt, compels the feeler to do certain things, often interpreted to be an expression of affection or caring. Not bad. The problem is that while I do a lot of things for other people that would definitely be considered as caring or suggesting affection, I'm not sure that they are motivated by a feeling of love. Mostly I do things like that out of a sense of duty. Or, since I am in the health care industry, out of a need for a paycheck.

I do a lot of caring things for my husband, but oddly, I never feel like saying I love him, because I'm an honest person, and I'm not sure it's true. Such a statement should come from the heart, not from the head. If I have to think about saying it, then it would be a lie. Maybe.

Like Sherlock in the final episode where he is forced to say "I Love You" to Molly Hooper in order to prevent her from being blown up. Did he really mean it? She believed him, which was all that mattered in the end. Like Sherlock, I'm always on guard against the vulnerability of engaging in feelings. I guess I've been hurt a few times, isn't that the usual story line?

A song from "Fiddler on the Roof" inevitably comes into my head at this point whenever I travel down this line of thought. My Father loved "Fiddler on the Roof" and played the soundtrack hundreds of times when we were kids. A favorite number was this duet sung by the main character, Tevye, and his wife. It was called "Do You Love Me?" Tevye and his wife Golde were wedded in the traditional fashion- arranged by their parents. They have five daughters who are now going off and finding husbands of their own. When one of the daughters defies him to run off and marry a poor tailor, Tevye doesn't understand why his daughter would make such a poor decision. "Because I love him," the daughter tells her father, "and he loves me." Tevye is stunned. He thinks about it and finally decides to consult his wife, Golde. "Golde," he demands, "do you love me?"
"Do I WHAT?" She screeches back.

I heard the recording a thousand times, growing up. So the duet between Tevye and Golde is pretty much engraved in my brain, and somehow captures my relationship with Hank. It goes like this:

(Tevya)
Do you love me?

(Golde)
Do I what?

(Tevye)
Do you love me?

(Golde)

179

Do I love you?
With our daughters getting married
And this trouble in the town
You're upset, you're worn out
Go inside, go lie down!
Maybe it's indigestion...

(Tevye)
"Golde I'm asking you a question..."

Do you love me?

(Golde)
You're a fool

(Tevye)
"I know..."

But do you love me?

(Golde)
Do I love you?
For twenty-five years I've washed your clothes
Cooked your meals, cleaned your house
Given you children, milked YOUR cow
After twenty-five years, why talk about love right now?

(Tevye)
Golde, The first time I met you
Was on our wedding day
I was scared

(Golde)
I was shy

(Tevye)
I was nervous

(Golde)
So was I

(Tevye)
But my father and my mother
Said we'd learn to love each other

And now I'm asking, Golde
Do you love me?

(Golde)
I'm your wife

(Tevye)
"I know..."
But do you love me?

(Golde)
Do I love him?
For twenty-five years I've lived with him
Fought with him, starved with him
Twenty-five years my bed is his
If that's not love, what is?

(Tevye)
Then you love me?

(Golde)
I suppose I do

(Tevye)
And I suppose I love you too

(Both)
It doesn't change a thing
But even so
After twenty-five years
It's nice to know.

I imagine this scene played out by Hank and I. Hank has a beautiful voice. I screech. It's not much of a leap to hear him singing the lyric "But, do you love me?" We've been together almost 25 years. I've done all the necessary things to take care of him, feed him, pay the bills, look after our dog-children, and maintain the property. He has an easy life in a warm cozy house. He's well fed, arguably coddled, and has everything he wants or needs. Like Golde I sing "If that's not love, what is?" Then Hank would be reassured: "then you love me." I guess I do, (but sometimes I wonder whether I just have an uber sense of duty.) It's a very sweet duet. Everyone is happy, for a while.

Ours is not a perfect marriage, but mostly we're good for each other and get along, and that's good enough for me, for now. I wouldn't mess it up for a sandwich, even a magical egg sandwich.

September 20, 2016

Day 18
Stratton

Don't ask me why I decided to stay in the shelter instead of finding a nice quiet private spot for my tent. I took a chance that no one would be coming in after me to the unoccupied Spruce Peak Shelter, and besides, the tent was still wet and I wanted to hang it up on the front porch of the lean-to. But at the last minute, as the last remnants of daylight were fading into dusk, a hiker came huffing and puffing up the access trail to the shelter. She was an AT hiker, southbound, a tiny young woman with enormous spirit and strength matched by an enormous pack which towered over her head. She'd come 20 some-thing miles today, pushing to get herself south before the weather turned cold. Despite the strenuous exertions she was facing, King Arthur, as she called herself, loved being on the trail. She never wanted to go back to real life, she said, "it sucks!" I empathized. I was glad enough to have King Arther's company for the evening, but I was restless most of the night, tossing and turning on my resonant air mattress on the hollow wooden echo chamber sleeping platform, worrying about disturbing my shelter-mate, and thinking about the day ahead. It was 11 miles to Stratton- would I make it in time for my lunch date? Was it too much to hope for that he would actually show up? Should I have asked him to throw in a couple of jars of peanut butter and a bag of bagels? No, that was too much. What if I was late- would he leave the food or give it to someone else?

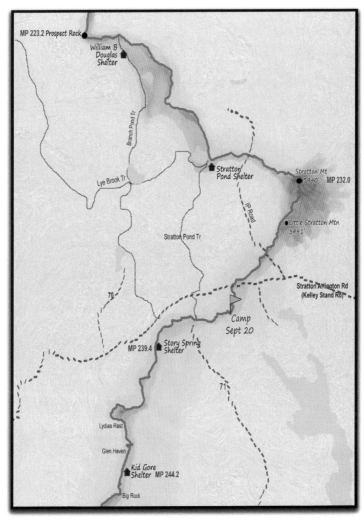

Map 14: Stratton

183

I got up early and started shaking out my gear and folding it up to stuff into my pack. The tent was still damp, but it was a lot drier and cleaner than it had been yesterday. I fed the girls and worked quickly through my usual morning routine, but Young King Arthur beat me onto the trail by 20 minutes despite having gotten up a half hour later than me. Dwarfed by her massive pack, she wished me a good hike and disappeared down the trail. I hoped she had a good journey and found whatever she was looking for. Then Lyssa, Tina and I headed south too.

We made good time. Spurred on by the prospect of real food for lunch we zoomed up the grade to Prospect Rock, barely nodding as we zipped past the turn-off for Manchester Center where a large re-supply box of provisions was waiting for us at the Manchester Post Office. That was for an alternate reality. Turning east and then southeast, we tromped along through swampy, unremarkable moderate elevation forest and arrived at the famous Stratton Pond. It was pretty, of course, but I was more impressed by the Stratton Pond Shelter, which was a marvel of alpine log cabin architecture. It was 11 am, I only had 3 miles to go to reach the summit of Stratton Mountain and I was starving. Three miles and 1,500 feet of climbing. Crossing my fingers that my angel from Bromley would come through with his promise, I pulled all of my rations for the day out of my pack and scarfed them down- a bag of tuna, two granola bars and some dried fruit and nuts. I was still hungry but I could face the climb ahead.

While I was eating I pulled out my phone and checked in with another alternate reality, the one I had left behind but would soon be going back to. To my surprise Stratton Pond shelter had a strong cell signal. I downloaded my email and found urgent messages from my brother Glenn and our real estate agent in South Carolina regarding the sale of my parents' old house. "'Bout time," I muttered to no one. I'd ordered the appraisal in July and signed a contract before I left. "You could have had this all done a month ago." Nothing happens quickly in the South. I called Glenn and the agent and we settled on the details for putting the house on the market. Then I finished my last granola bar and sent up a prayer to the Universe that the house would sell before I finished my hike. End of alternate reality intrusion. We headed for Stratton Mountain.

After a mile or so we arrived at a small clear flowing creek and I stopped to check the map. As far as I could tell this was the only certain water source for the next 10 miles or so; I'd play it safe and tank up. I was digging out the bottle and filters when Lyssa started barking her serious guard dog alert bark. She didn't do it very often, so I dropped my gear and went to investigate. A hiker was approaching up the trail from behind us, a big guy with braces on both knees, moving strong and fast. Lyssa was wary about letting him get too close to me. I grabbed her collar and told her I had things under control, just as my trainer had taught us. She sat and I apologized to the man, who didn't seem bothered. He stopped and took off his pack by the creek, and I asked him about his hike. He was doing the AT, he said, one state at a time. He was almost finished with Vermont. There was something deeply familiar about the way he spoke, and as his voice trickled down through my head I began to hear the voices of my grandparents and the old aunts and uncles from my Mom's side of the family. "Philadelphia," I said. "You're from Philadelphia!"

Bingo! The big man from Philadelphia laughed and relaxed a little. With as many relatives as I had in southeast Pennsylvania he might well have been a fourth or fifth cousin. We chatted about the trail and his knee problems, and he asked me if I knew anything about the trail-head at the Massachusetts State line. There were two options- you could go to Williamstown via the Pine Cobble Trail, or stay on the AT and come out in North Adams. Philadelphia man was desperate to find a store where he could buy a charger for his phone, hopefully with a hotel nearby. I dug out my guidebook and looked up accommodations in Williamstown, and found a trail-friendly hotel that offered ride-service to hikers to and from the Pine Cobble Trail-head. It sounded a lot preferable to the North Adams option, where the trail was routed across some busy urban streets in a semi-industrialized section of town. The North Adams trail-head was not a safe place to leave a car, according to the book. It didn't sound inviting. "Look, you can call this hotel and ask them about stores that carry phone equipment. If you call now I bet you could even get a reservation for a room and arrange for a ride," I suggested. Philadelphia-Man thought that sounded like a great idea if only his stupid his phone hadn't been dead for three days. He hadn't even been able to check in with his family, he said, irritably. I could sympathize with that dilemma. But I'd found the solution: I had a couple of spare portable phone charging batteries with a USB ports for the cable. *Pay it forward said my trail angel.* "Would you like a charge?" Words came out of my mouth. "My husband mailed me a couple of these bat-

Stratton Mountain Lookout Tower has a fantastic view of southern Vermont

teries so that I wouldn't run out of juice, but I won't need both of them." He hesitated about my offer- it was too good to be true. "You'd be doing me a favor by taking one, if it will work for you. I need to lighten my pack and every little bit helps." I could see relief flooding into his face. He jotted down the phone number of the hotel and dug out his phone and a cable, and I went back to filling my water bottles. When his phone lit up and started dinging with messages from his family, the girls and I headed on up the trail for our lunch date on Stratton Mountain. An hour later Philadelphia caught up with me halfway up the steep final ascent of Stratton. This time Lyssa gave him her usual happy dog hello, and he responded cheerfully. "I got my reservation and a ride to Walmarts" he said, zipping past me. "Thanks for everything!"

I decided I liked this Pay it Forward thing- it almost felt as good as a magical egg sandwich!

When I was in about 6th grade my family took a ski vacation to Stratton Mountain. We had lace up boots, wooden skis, polyester filled parkas with big flowers on them, and homemade hats, mittens and scarves. Dad took us all the way to the top on the chairlift- I remember an unearthly winter wonderland where the wind had created magical snow sculptures around the spruces at the summit. Grinding up the backside of Stratton Mountain with my girls, I wondered if anything would look familiar. Nothing did. The tower at the top is awesome to climb up, especially when you first peek above the canopy and get a look at the mountains and valleys all around you. In summer Vermont is a gorgeous, luscious, green/pristine state. My Angel from New Jersey met me at the summit. This time he had two egg sandwiches and bacon for the girls, and I have no doubt that Angels are real and they are watching over us. "Pay it forward," he said again. I will. I started by taping up the open blisters on his heels with first aid cream and moleskin. I'm good at bandages. That night we camped at Black Brook, near Story Spring Shelter and feasted on egg sandwich #2 and bacon. Lucky, happy, full-bellied campers, watched over by a host of a angels.

We had 3 days and 39 miles left to go. 39 miles didn't seem like much but it would still take 3 days and every bit of my energy reserves to do it. 39 miles was less than my daily round trip commute, and less than the distance from my house to Lake Tahoe. It was nothing compared to the 4,000 mile drive back to my home on the west coast. But it was still a 3 day march- maybe not the most strenuous days I'd done, but to be honest I was feeling tired. Depleted. I was pretty much running on sheer willpower the last few hours to Black Brook. I was skinny, grubby, thoroughly damp and a little shivery going through the evening routine- setting up the tent, feeding my girls, laying out my sleeping bag and mattress. In the low lying creek basin the air was cool and clammy and the light was dim. I missed the sunshine and warm dry air of the Sierras! I cocooned myself in my down pants and sweater and pulled out my treasured egg sandwich in it's beautiful crumpled foil wrapper and ate it slowly, savoring every bite. Did my angel have any idea what a gift he'd given me? I had no way to tell him. I could do 39 miles, no problem.

Only 3 more cozy nights in my little tent with my beautiful beloved furry companions. I loved my tent. When I set it up it suddenly defined a space that was all mine (and Tina's and Lyssa's) and it was our home. I could put it anywhere, and it would be home- safe, cozy and familiar. Just the three of us. I would seriously miss my tent. It would end suddenly. I'd take the last step and cross the finish line. There would be no more trail ahead of me. We'd just get in Dale's car and drive away. First we'd fetch my package from the Manchester Post Office and then we'd head for Waitsfield and spend the night at the ski lodge. I'd take a long hot shower and then we'd go to dinner- I wanted pasta with rich creamy Alfredo sauce and a giant salad with Italian dressing, and bread with thick slabs of butter. And a beer. I'd drink 2 pints of Long

Trail Ale; one because it was Long Trail Ale and another because it tasted so darn good. Then another hot shower before I lost consciousness in my bunk at the lodge.

Only 39 miles and 3 days of simplicity and freedom of from responsibility other than watching out for my dogs and putting one foot in front of the other. Of time to let my mind wander freely wherever it willed. 3 more days of total immersion in nature, forest, mountains and fresh air, of me and co-travelers joined by invisible bonds, like 3 entangled particles crawling over our humble planet, our home in the universe. I wasn't in any hurry to finish. When I shed my pack I would replace it with heavier and more cumbersome burdens- I had work to do. Things would change- I would make them change- because I wouldn't go back to letting things be the way they had been before. It would take time, but I knew I could do it. I'd finish settling my parents' estate and start getting the clinic ready to hand over to the next generation of young veterinarians. I'd get our financial ducks in a row, and then... then... I'd take care of me!

Hadn't that always been the plan? Perhaps, but the problem was that I really didn't know what it meant to take care of me.

What would life look like if I gave myself permission to do things that I wanted to do , and NOT do things that I didn't want to do or did out of a sense of obligation or service to others. What would it be like to accept things the way they were and not try to fix everything for everyone? I didn't know. Did I want to move to Vermont? I didn't know. It would be an awful lot of work to do it, so I had better be sure, with clear and compelling reasons. What I really wanted was freedom. Freedom to spend time walking with my dogs, time to wander around pretty places with my camera taking photographs and time to spend sorting and editing the photos, writing down my thoughts and stories about the places I went and things I saw- ideas, perceptions, insights and inspirations about my journey. I wanted to record all of the things I found interesting and beautiful and worth sharing about the world. I wanted freedom from stress and obligation. I wanted to be able to take time off from work to putter in my garden, cultivating vegetables, flowers and maybe even get into propagating native plants. I wanted to live someplace where there was enough water to grow things, where there was plenty of rain and where lakes and creeks didn't dry up and turn to dust. I wasn't sure I could handle snow and cold, but maybe it wouldn't be so bad. I needed more information. I'll come back in February, I decided, and spend a week in Vermont in the winter. I had some money coming from the estate and it might be enough to buy an acceptable property in Vermont. How much equity could we expect from our house in California? It was nearly paid off. I hated the thought of selling it but we'd need money for the move and there would always be maintenance expenses. We'd need to make sure we had enough to pay contractors and carpenters since our "do-it-yourself" days were pretty much over. I'd probably have to keep working. Oops, that was a problem! Could I find the type of work I liked in Vermont? Was there even such a thing as shelter work or spay/ neuter clinics. I didn't think pet overpopulation was much of an issue here. Maybe I could retire and do something else entirely. We could buy a place with a guest house and run a bed & breakfast- that sounded easy enough. Right. I couldn't imagine Hank playing the congenial host, much less helping to clean and maintain the place. And what about the dogs? Wed need fences and plenty of acreage so that it wouldn't bother neighbors when they barked. Would I be able to take them running in the forest the way I do now? At home we can go off leash out the back gate and down into the canyon- it's all National Forest land and we have our own private trails! It sure was getting complicated and stressful, and the point of the whole idea was to simplify and reduce stress! I had to keep thinking.

Chapter 10

September 21, 2016

Day 19
Glastenbury Mountain

I woke up early, still thinking, and kept on thinking while I served out the breakfast rations, packed up the gear and hit the trail. All morning long I pushed and thought and kept walking and kept thinking. I only had 3 days left to figure it out. I wanted it to be over so that I could rest, but more than anything else I wanted to finish the Trail. I couldn't explain why, but I was obsessed with completing every step of the trail from Canada to Massachusetts. It was as if one obsession, the death of my parents, had been replaced with another obsession- finishing the trail. I was driving myself to finish just as I had driven myself to take care of them, and at no less sacrifice to my own health and well-being.

All the way from Black Brook to Glastenbury summit I tromped and thought, pushing my tired and depleted body as if somehow the state of utter exhaustion could bring clarity to my thoughts, as if when all of the noise and obfuscation was left behind the thing that remained would be the truth, naked and obvious. I drove myself without stopping to Glastenbury summit, dropping my pack and climbing up the rickety stairs to the top of the lookout tower. The answer was out there if only I could get high enough, above the treetops, above the canopy and above all of the distrac-

MP 248 Fire Tower ● Glastenbury Mtn
3748'

Goddard
Shelter

Glastenbury Lookout

3331'

Little Pond Lookout

Porcupine
MP 254 Lookout

Camp Sept. 21

Maple Hill
2690'

Melville
Nauheim
Shelter

Split Rock

9

Harmon Hill MP 260.2
2325'

Map 15: Glastenbury Mtn to Harmon Hill

tions. I saw only rolling hills in every direction. Beautiful emerald green hills, dotted with blue lakes and ponds, with blue skies and scattered puffy white clouds overhead. A clean, pristine, gorgeous landscape. I tried to imagine it cold and frozen, covered in snow, icy winds blowing across dreary dead meadows. I couldn't do it. I only loved it as it was on that 21st day of September when the gentle warm mantle of summer still lay lightly on the land.

Glastenbury Mountain was the highest point of the day's hike and the last real summit of the trip. After Glastenbury I could relax a little, knowing that I was over the hump in terms of dialing in my mileage goal for the day.

I am surprised when I see my first acorns on the trail- here be oak trees! I haven't seen oaks since I left our home in the foothills. Seeing them makes me feel like I really am getting closer to home. Soon we will be at the Southern Terminus and the hike will be over. I've been so focused on the Trail and doing this hike that I haven't really had time to think about home. It seems so very far away- like, across more than just a continent- like, across the whole dang galaxy. Having Tina and Lyssa with me has prevented me from feeling homesick or lonely. In fact, I haven't felt lonely for an instant. I wonder if the dogs miss home at all. They seem happy- they race up and down the trail and sniff all the interesting scents and investigate everything there is to investigate, much as they did on the first day of the trip. Lyssa still pounces enthusiastically on anything that squeaks or scurries, although she is getting better about paying more attention when she is on leash and not jerking me off my feet. Progress has been slow but we keep working on it. In fact, I think Lyssa could go on this way for the rest of her life. She is lean and lanky and muscular and never runs out of energy, even on these long 18 mile days. Tina is as acrobatic and perky as ever. Whenever I have Lyssa on the leash, which is often in these open southern chipmunk-in-

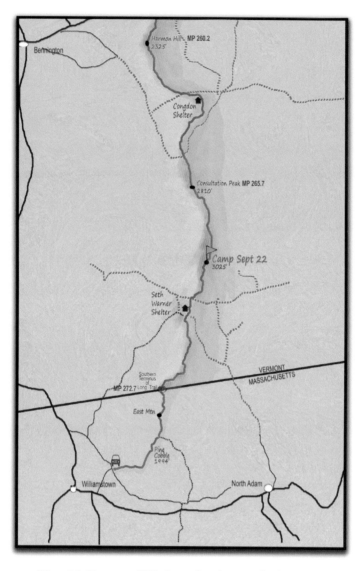

Map 16: Harmon Hill, Consultation Peak, the Southern Terminus, and the Pine Cobble Trail

*fested forests, Tina seizes the chance to forge ahead and
take over as trail-blazer. She even does a little pouncing,
which she normally leaves up to big sister.*

*Somewhere near "Porcupine Lookout" both dogs suddenly
got very excited for no apparent reason. Tina ran back
and forth through the forest, barking, and Lyssa, who was
on leash because dogs and porcupines don't mix well, was
almost impossible for me to hang onto. As I fought for
control, (and won), I suddenly realized that there was a
peculiar barnyard-like smell in the air. Cows? Not likely!
Just then a hiker approaching from below stopped and ten-
tatively inquired whether everything was okay (deranged
lady with giant crazed beast tied to her waist....) I shouted
that I was fine but my dog had just lost her mind because
there was a moose in the neighborhood. Approaching cautiously, he noticed the smell too- definitely livestock-like!
Wow! Smelling a moose is almost better than seeing one!
I kept Lyssa tied close to me the rest of the day and through
the night, although she regained her senses as soon as we
put some distance between us and Moose territory. Not
homesick, these dogs. Moose! This is the life! Love this Trail!*

We camped at a tiny streamlet just south of Porcupine
Hill. The spot was too close to the trail but it was clear
and level and just barely big enough for the tent. It was
getting dark and I knew that no more hikers would be
coming by. Plus we'd be gone in the morning by the time
it was light enough to see the trail. We were heading
home.

September 22, 2016
Day 20

Harmon Hill

*It's finally arrived- our last full day of hiking on the Long
Trail. I will miss the simplicity of this life-- freed of the
usual worries and responsibilities of my normal existence.*

I will miss the cozy companionship of having only 2 dogs to share my attention. I will miss the strenuous daily physical workout. I will miss the forest, the trees, rocks, moss, ferns, mushrooms, salamanders, brooks, ponds and bogs. Not the mud. Lyssa will miss the chipmunks, no doubt, although they won't miss her. As for Tina, she's always in the moment!

Today is the last full day I have for walking and thinking. I'm desperate to figure out the answer by the time I cross the Massachusetts state line. I want all the pieces tied together in a tidy package and wrapped up with a bow on top. Today is the day for my "Eureka moment".
On the way up and over Maple Hill I noticed that something was wrong with my leg muscles. Climbing up the hill they felt weak, flaring with fatigue at every step, and I had to slow down to a crawl as if I was at 10,000 feet elevation instead of 2,500. On they way down my quads were cramping, screaming in pain and threatening to lock up. I stopped at Melville Nauheim Shelter for coffee, a granola bar and an ibuprofen. Ibuprofen upsets my stomach and causes an ulcer, but I needed to be able to keep walking. Anti-inflammatories were indicated. There was a steep downhill ahead and an even steeper climb uphill on the south side of route 9. The rest of the trail was going to be a piece of cake- I just needed a little help for now, I thought. I briefly considered the possibility that the non-stop 17 & 18 mile days were catching up to me, and that I was pushing too hard and needed to rest, but I told myself that I should be getting used to it by now. I was in great shape- no pain, no gain! Besides, I almost there- less than 20 miles to the finish line. I could rest later.

Southbound, we roll. Across Hell Hollow Brook, over Maple Hill, past Mr. Melville Nauheim shelter, and steeply down to Highway 9. The workmanship on the stone staircases is impressive, reminding me of the stone staircases I have traversed in the Sierras. Rockbound Pass, Desolation Wilderness, The John Muir Trail, Yosemite. They seem dry and barren of life compared to the Green Mountains, like those photos of Mars- so inhospitable. But while the Western Mountains are as stunning as they are stark and rocky, they are no more or less grand and exhilarating than this climb up Harmon Hill! Harmon Hill. An appropriate place to pause, rest and reflect. I only need to hike 8 & 1/2 miles today to be in a strategic spot for finishing the trek tomorrow. I came to Vermont to hike because I wanted to get away from the drought, heat and fires in California. I wanted to be immersed in this green verdant land. In the back of my mind I am nursing the notion of running away from the hot dry dusty west- a climate refugee- and I like what I see in Vermont. But to relocate my family here would take monumental effort, and so I would have to be absolutely sure. I'm not sure- I have only seen Vermont in the summer. There are 3 other Vermonts- Fall, Winter and Spring- that give me pause: a stop-dead-in-my-tracks kind of pause! Although I have often mused that my husband would be happy anywhere there was a warm living room with good wifi and a well stocked kitchen full of snacks, he does not, in fact, do well in cold, damp, cloudy conditions. He's a born and bred Westerner. I enjoy skiing and snow-shoeing, but my fingers and toes are exquisitely sensitive to frostbite, and I'm not so sure about all the mud with which Vermont is well endowed. Would it be wise to escape fire and drought for cold, wet and cloudy? The answer was not on Harmon Hill, although I did enjoy the rest and the view! Silly me, thinking that I was on a downhill run to the finish line. Trail was not through with me yet! After the summit of Harmon Hill we did not descend. No sir. After a bit of not climbing we started climbing again, and then proceeded to roller coaster along past Congdon Camp and through the boggy bottom lands of Stamford Creek, past Sucker Pond. One of my aspirations for the day was to get as clean and de-stinkified as I could for my return to civilization. Sucker Pond, however, was not an inviting option for a bath. It wasn't until several more long ups, (and short downs), that

I crossed Roaring Branch and realized that the time had come. I was as sweaty and stinky as I would ever be and it was the warmest part of the day for drying off, and best of all I had the luxury of having more time than miles left in the day. There's a fine art to taking a bath in a brook with only a nalgene bottle of water and a few drops of biodegradable soap. You wash one limb at a time, being careful not to drop any suds in the brook, all the while staying discreetly hidden downstream so as not to shock any passing hikers. The dogs made themselves comfortable by the water while I scrubbed. An hour later, much refreshed and tolerably un-smelly, we continued on. At peak 3025 we stopped for the night. The guidebook promised views, but was obviously written before the grove of dwarf oak trees had grown up on the summit. Moose and deer tracks abounded, so Lyssa stayed safely on leash and out of temptation.

It was the last night on the trail. We were going to make it. I could see the light at the end of the tunnel, or maybe it was the light at the end of the re-birth canal. My obsessive/ compulsive marathon sprint across the last 100 miles was almost over; the end was within reach, but I was no closer to having an answer to my question about what my new life would look like. The only thing that was clear was that I never wanted to push myself this hard again. Why did I do it? Why did I feel so driven to finish the trail like I did? Was it pride, the source of unrealistic expectations about myself and my abilities? Am I just doomed to be obsessive and goal driven in everything I do? I'd been compulsively goal driven for so long- working overtime to meet our financial needs, taking care of my parents and putting my life on hold to shepherd them through their final few years of life, efficiently meeting all of the needs of all of the animals that came through the clinic. The obvious conclusion was that I had simply glommed onto another goal and I had no choice but to give it my every last ounce of effort in order to succeed. It's just how I was wired. But this felt different. It was

Shirley Harman lives in Northern California. You can read more of her essays on traveling and hiking with dogs at http://sixdogstudios.com.

Afterward

In the fall of 2016 rain returned to Northern California. That winter the Sierras were buried under 200% of the normal precipitation for the season and the authorities reluctantly concluded that the drought was over. We still have to be careful about conserving, they said, but you could water your garden again.

Hank and I talked about moving somewhere cooler and greener, where life could be simpler and less stressful, but in the end we decided there wasn't anyplace better than the west slope of the northern Sierra Nevada mountains. I threw myself into a mission to recruit and train some new young veterinarians to take over the clinic for me, which proved to be easier said than done, but someday soon I will be free to go and do as I please.

I walk the dogs a lot, but never again will we go with the goal of attaining some distant finish line just for the sake of finishing. Now I walk because I like to be outside walking on the earth, and I appreciate the beautiful things to be found under my nose. I may do another long distance hike because there are so many great trails and places to go. The journey may be the goal, but, for me, the best goal is no goal at all!

Have a good hike.

November 21, 2017
Pollock Pines

The End